新装版 「工場管理」基本と実践シリーズ

英語で kaizen! トヨタ生産方式

成沢俊子 with John Shook—著

Kaizen Express

日刊工業新聞社

本書は日刊工業新聞社発行『英語でkaizen!　トヨタ生産方式―第2版―』
の新装版として発行したものです。

はじめに
Introduction

本書は、月刊誌「工場管理」の連載「なんて言えばいいの？ KAIZEN」(2005年10月号〜2007年5月号) をもとにまとめたものです。単行本化に際し、John Shook氏より幅広く深い助言を得ました。本書はLean Enterprise Institute (LEI) の研究成果から多くを引用して成り立っています。本書出版にあたり、LEIの創立者でありチェアマンであるWomack博士に深く感謝申し上げます。

海外工場の人々に改善を伝える仕事に初めて出会ったのは、1990年代半ばのことでした。当然のように自身の英語力不足を痛感する日々でしたが、同時に、単に英語にするだけでは伝えきれない何かがあることにも気づいていました。時を経て、2005年の秋から再び中国と東南アジアの工場を頻繁に訪れる機会を得た私は、海外工場で改善を教えなければならない日本の製造業の人々がずいぶんたくさんいることを知るようになりました。今日、日本の大きな企業にとって、海外生産は当たり前と言えるくらいになっており（すでに空洞化の議論を越え、所与の条件になっているとさえ言えるかもしれません）、またそれゆえ、海外工場の生産性向上は日本人にとっても重要な課題です。低賃金の労働力という見方だけで海外生産をとらえているなら、早晩行き詰ってしまうでしょう。加えて、人・モノ・エネルギーのムダ遣いを世界的規模で改善すべきであることは論を俟たないはずです。

Shook氏の手になる"Learning to See[1]"を翻訳して以来、多くの方から「英語のよい教材を教えて」とたずねられ、LEIのワークブックシリーズや用語集[2] を紹介してきましたが、「やはり英語だけでは使いにくい」というのが筆者を含む普通の日本人の本音でもありました。「工場管理」編集長の矢島氏（当時）から連載のお話をいただいた時、このような内容なら多くの人の役に立つのではと考えたのは上述の経験からです。本書の構成は、海外工場で「座学＋実践」のセッションを何回かに分けて行う場合の対訳教材として、そのまま使えるように考えました。読者の皆さんは、国内の工場で、おそらく同じような構成のトレーニングを経験されているものと想像していましたが、海外でもそれをやってみたいと考える人が予想以上に多いことを連載中に知り、本書では生産管理板をはじめとする基本的なフォームのいくつかを追加しました。

連載中、構成・内容ともに、海外の改善の仲間と交わした会話から多くの着想を得ました。彼らとの対話なしには、この連載を続けることはできなかったでしょう。ちょうど連載期間と重なるこの間、一緒に改善に取り組んでくれた海外工場の皆さん、その機会を与えてくださった企業の皆さんに、この場をお借りして御礼申し上げます。もとより、海外工場で改善を学ぶ機会を下さったのはPEC産業教育センター所長の山田日登志先生です。トヨタ生産方式をどのように学ぶかについて、長い間ご指導いただいてきましたこと、深く感謝申し上げます。

日刊工業新聞社出版局「工場管理」編集長の矢島俊克氏、平井瑛子氏には連載開始から現在まで、

多くの励ましをいただきました。本書の出版は、同局書籍編集部長・奥村功氏、同部・加藤真澄氏のお力によるものです。本書の出版に関わって下さった皆様方に、改めて御礼申し上げます。

ところで、トヨタ生産方式に学び、それを海外に持って行くということに関心のある方なら、トヨタ自動車の皆さんがどのようにそれを実行されたのかについても深い興味を抱いているはずです。筆者もその一人です。トヨタ生産方式の海外への伝播を追ううちに"Learning to See"と出会い、Shook氏を知るようになった筆者は彼を通して、1980年代前半からトヨタが気の遠くなるような努力を傾けて北米へ出て行ったことを知り、トヨタに対し改めて深い尊敬の念を抱くようになりました。Shook氏は80年代前半にトヨタ本社が正規社員として雇用した最初の（当時は唯一の）外国人でした。後に彼はトヨタ本社初の米国人管理職ともなるのですが、それはまさにNUMMI[3]の設立準備からケンタッキーへの本格進出の時期であり、後の世界展開の礎を築いた期間でもありました。この間、「トヨタのやり方」を米国へ（そしてその他の国々へ）持って行くために彼が果たした役割は非常に大きかったと想像します（Womack博士や、後のLiker教授他の研究に大きな影響を与えたことでも彼はよく知られています）。本書で紹介したトヨタ生産方式の英語表現のほとんどはShook氏とその仲間が続けてきた実践と考察に依拠しており、後学の徒として深い感謝を捧げるものです。もちろん英語表現のみならず彼らの実践自体も実に興味深く、筆者も多くを学んできました。しかしそ

れ以上に、Shook氏を最初に雇用したトヨタ人事部の慧眼、さらには、まず優秀なアメリカ人をトヨタ本社で採用しなければならないと考えたトップマネジメントこそ、おそるべしと言わねばならないでしょう。「トヨタのやり方」からすれば、当然の方針であり行動であったのかもしれません。そのもとをたどれば、やはり「トヨタのやり方」が人を基盤として成り立っていること、今も昔も一貫して人を尊重することをとても大切にしているということに行き着くのだろうと考えます。

筆者自身も含め、一般に、日本人は心のなかで人の気持ちを思いやることはできても、それを表に出すことは得意ではありません。「オープン・マインド」について、私たちは外国の人々から学ぶべきことがもっとあるように思うのです。海外工場での改善活動は、それを学ぶ得難いチャンスでもあるでしょう。本書が海外工場で改善を進めようとする読者の皆さんのお役に立てるのなら、とてもうれしいことです。皆さんの活動が、より楽しく、実りあるものでありますように！

2007年7月

成沢　俊子

1. Learning to See: LEI, 1998, 邦訳『トヨタ生産方式にもとづく『モノ』と『情報』の流れ図で現場の見方を変えよう！！』（日刊工業新聞社）
2. 用語集：Lean Lexicon (LEI, Version 3.0, September 2006)
3. NUMMI: New United Motor Manufacturing, Inc. トヨタ自動車とGMの合弁による自動車製造会社。1984年設立。在カリフォルニア州。

第2版の発行にあたり
Introduction to the Second Edition

継続的改善の精神に則り、「英語でkaizen! トヨタ生産方式」
（英語名：Kaizen Express）の第２版を皆さんにお届けすること
ができるのは幸いです。今回の改版では、多くの細かい改善
点に加え、簡潔で使いやすい教材を付録−２として追加しまし
た。読者の皆さんからのフィードバックをいただければ幸いで
す。皆さんが皆さん自身の改善の旅を続けるのと同じように、
私たちもまた本書の改善を続けたいと願っています。

成沢俊子、ジョン・シュック
2008年1月

In the spirit of continuous kaizen, we are pleased to introduce
this second edition of Kaizen Express. In addition to numerous
small improvements, we have added a new section of simple,
easy-to-use training materials as Appendix-2. We look forward
to your feedback - as you continue your own kaizen journey, we
will do the same with Kaizen Express!

T. Narusawa and J. Shook,
February, 2008

新装版 はじめに
Introduction

　このたびの新装版の刊行を、とてもうれしく思っています。

　2007年に本書の初版をつくったときの私たちの考えは、「トヨタ生産方式の基本のかたちを、多くの国の人々と一緒に学べたら、どんなに楽しいだろう」というものでした。爾来16年、Lean Enterprise InstituteとLean Global Networkの力によって、米国版、台湾版（繁体字）、ブラジル版、中国版（簡体字）、ハンガリー版、オランダ版、チリ版（スペイン語-ポルトガル語の対訳バージョン）などが次々に誕生しました。初版刊行時に思い描いていた夢が現実となり、さまざまな国で本書を愛し、活用いただいていることに深く感謝しています。

台湾版　　米国版　　中国版　　ブラジル版

タイのSurasak Fakumさん（左写真左）
モンクット王工科大学北バンコク校と支援先企業の皆さんに本書を贈呈してくださいました（2018年）

＊　＊　＊　＊　＊

　この間、世界のマネジメント論の世界では、かなり大きな変化が起きていたように思います。それは、機械論的な考え方（Mechanical Thinking）から、"Living-Systems Thinking"へという新潮流でした。Living-Systems Thinkingとは「組織は生き物」という見方、行動の仕方です。日本においても、かつての欧米流の機械論的マネジメントに表面が覆われているかのような時代がありましたが、日本企業のマネジメントの底流には「組織は生き物」という考え方が、ずっと存在していたように思われます。すばらしい企業ほど、そうでしょう。

　本書の初版において私たちは「トヨタ生産方式の基本形を言語ニュートラルな表現で描き出す」ことを狙っていました。その反面、トヨタ生産方式のメカニカルな側面、テクニカルな側面に読者の焦点を向けるものであったかもしれません。

　しかし、「これが基本の形だからやりなさい」と押し付けられて、はたして人は幸せになれるでしょうか。

　職場を、現場をよくしていくために、改善の基本形が大切なのは当然のことながら、いわゆるソーシャル・スキル、仲間と心を合わせて日々の活動を進めていくスキルなしに定着は困難です。この面での研究が近年深まり、知見が広がっていくのを見るのは、私たちにとって、ありがたい経験

でした。

＊　＊　＊　＊　＊

　"トヨタ式"が世界的に注目を集めるようになった1980年代以降、ずいぶん長い間、人々は「トヨタ式改善に取り組んで、大きな成果が出た。しかし、しばらくすると、後戻りしてしまう。我々の知らない、何か足りないピースがあるのではないか」という「足りないピース探しの旅」を続けてきました。そうして辿り着いた１つの気づきが「足りないピースは私たちの心の中にあったのだ」という、言うなれば当たり前の教訓であったのかもしれません。

　１人ひとりの発見、感動、共感といった心のはたらきが、組織にどれほど強い影響をあたえていることか。

　脳科学や生物学の研究成果がLiving-Systems Thinkingへの人々の理解を促した面もあるでしょう。最近では、ヒトに限らず、あらゆる生物においてコミュニケーションと共感の能力が種の繁栄と深く関わっているという研究が行なわれ、人々の関心を集めています。

　人を理解するための学びに終わりはなく、これからもさまざまな仮説が提示され、実験を通して検証されていくことでしょう。

＊　＊　＊　＊　＊

　私たちは、そうした仮説検証の学びのサイクルに、１つの実践的な「枠組み」を生み出したのが

トヨタだと考えています。

　この「枠組み」は、トヨタ生産方式として、あるいは「トヨタのTQC」として、世界中で研究され、今では多くの人が知るものとなりましたが、大切なのは、現地現物で、実践を通してのみ、本物の学びが生まれるという点です。

　いま、この瞬間にも、さまざまな産業のいろいろな現場で新たな発見があり、驚きがあり、仲間と共に学び続けている人がたくさんいるはずです。

　これからも、本書がそうした学びの旅の助けとなれるなら、著者としてこれに勝るよろこびはありません。

2023年１月
成沢俊子／ジョン・シュック

Chapter 1

初めて学ぶトヨタ生産方式
Let's Learn TPS

Chapter 2

ジャスト・イン・タイム
Just-in-Time with Flow, Pull and Heijunka

Chapter 3

自働化と設備改善
Jidoka and Machines

Kaizen Express

Chapter 4　工程の安定化
Process Stability

Chapter 5　改善に終わりなし
The Lean Journey

付録-1　改善フォーム集
Forms

Kaizen Express

CONTENTS

 付録-2 プリント教材
Training Materials

ワードリスト＆索引
Word List & Index

Chapter 1

初めて学ぶトヨタ生産方式
Let's Learn TPS

初めて学ぶトヨタ生産方式 ── 1
Let's Learn TPS

ムダとは？
What is Waste?

ムダをひとことで言うと？─MUDA＝"Waste"

トヨタ生産方式の教本では「付加価値を生み出さないで、原価のみを高める生産の諸要素」。
しかし、これをそのまま英語にすると、硬い表現になってしまいます。

そこでムダとは、　MUDA?
顧客にとっての価値を生み出さないのに、資源を消費しているもの、状態。
Any activity that consumes resources without creating value for the customer.

あるいは、　or
顧客が喜んで「お金を払いたい」とは思わないようなもの、状態。
Any activity for which the customer is not willing to pay.

と説明すると、英語圏の人にはわかりやすくなるようです。

◇7つのムダ ······················· Seven Wastes

大野耐一氏は、現場のムダを7つに分類しました。

Mr. Taiichi Ohno's categorization of the seven major wastes typically found at any gemba (workplace):

①つくり過ぎのムダ············ Overproduction

顧客や後工程が要求している量・タイミング・速度よりも、多く、早く、速く、つくってしまうこと。

Producing more, sooner or faster than is required by the next process or customer.

②手待ちのムダ ·················· Waiting

いきなり「標準作業の作業順序に従って仕事をする過程で…」と始めても、なかなかわかってもらえません。最初に説明するときは、なるべく簡単に。

動作のムダの見方

Categories of Work Motion Diagram

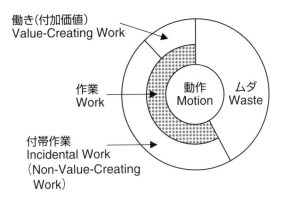

働き（付加価値）
Value-Creating Work

作業
Work

動作
Motion

ムダ
Waste

付帯作業
Incidental Work
（Non-Value-Creating
Work）

作業者が何もせずに何かを待っていること。マシンサイクル待ちや設備の復旧待ち、部品の遅れ待ちなど。

Operators standing idle as machines cycle, equipment fails, parts delay, etc.

③運搬のムダ

Conveyance

運搬はそれ自体がムダ。なぜなら、付加価値をまったく生まないから。もちろん、部品や製品は運ばざるを得ませんが、運搬のムダは最小限にしなくてはいけません。

Conveyance itself is waste because it creates no value. Obviously parts and products must be transported, but any movement beyond the absolute minimum is MUDA.

④加工そのもののムダ

Processing (or Overprocessing)

必要のない加工、正しくない加工。

Unnecessary or incorrect processing.

⑤在庫のムダ

Inventory

余分な材料、部品、仕掛品、完成品を持つこと。さらに正確に言えば、きちっと運用されている後工程引取り方式において、決められた量よりも、多く持つこと。

Keeping unnecessary raw materials, parts, WIP (work in process) and finished goods. More precisely, keeping more than the minimum stock necessary for a well-controlled pull system.

⑥動作のムダ

Motion

作業者の動作のうち、付加価値を生まないもの。作業者のみならず、機械の動きの中にも、動作のムダを見つけることができる。

Operator making movements that is creating no value. We can also identify waste in the motion of machines.

⑦不良をつくるムダ

Correction

検査、手直し、不良の廃棄。

Inspection, rework and scrap.

 役立つムダの分類

停滞のムダと、動作・運搬のムダ

ムダの発見と廃除には、次の2つのムダの分類がとても役立ちます。
Try looking for it from these view points;

1 モノに着目した、**停滞のムダ**
See stops, delays or accumulation by focusing on the flow of the product.

2 動きに着目した、**動作・運搬のムダ**
See non-value-creating motion by focusing on movement of people and machines.

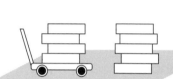

 ワンポイントレッスン **1**

ムラ、ムリ、ムダを語りたい

ムラ、ムリ、ムダを3点セットで語りたいとき、どうしますか？　ムラがあるからムリをする、ムリをするからムダが出る、などにピッタリの対応語は、残念ながらまだ発見されていないようです。ムラは"fluctuation"、ムリは"overburden"。

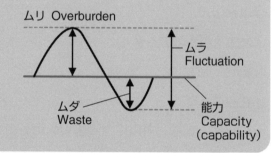

ワンポイントレッスン **2**

カタカナのムダとひらがなのむだ

さすがに、カタカナ、ひらがなまでは英語で表現できません。こんなときは、ムダには2つのタイプがあり、1つはすぐに取れるムダ（can be eliminated quickly by kaizen）と、もう1つはすぐには取れないむだ（cannot be eliminated immediately）であると説明した上で、それぞれの例（工程間の間締めですぐに取れる停滞や運搬の「ムダ」、不良の真因を取り除かなくては解決しない手直しの「むだ」など）を挙げます。

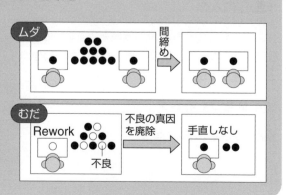

Overproduction
つくり過ぎ

Let's talk

つくり過ぎに気付こう！

A：つくり過ぎは最も悪いムダです。

B：どうして？

A：つくり過ぎは、その他のいろいろなムダのもととなり、ムダを見えなくしてしまうから。たとえば、在庫や不良、余計な運搬。

B：ということは、私たちの現場にもつくり過ぎのムダがある？

A：その通り。工程 X と工程 y の間に、仕掛りがあるでしょう？　これがつくり過ぎです。いくつありますか？

B：10個です。どうすればよいですか？

A：X と y の間を詰める。そして、仕掛りを1つに保つのです。どうですか？

B：y の作業が終わるまで X が手待ちになります。

A：タクトタイムは何秒？　タクトタイムに合わせて1人で作業するか、または作業を再配分してはどうですか？

A：Overproduction is the worst form of waste.

B：Why?

A：Because it generates and hides other wastes, such as inventory, defects and excess transport.

B：So, do you think we are also doing "overproduction" at our workplace?

A：Exactly! There is some WIP between process x and process y. That is the waste of overproduction. How many pieces are there?

B：Ten pieces. How do we eliminate them?

A：Let's connect the two processes, then keep just one piece between x and y. How about this kaizen?

B：The operator of x is waiting until y completes the cycle.

A：What is the takt time? How about trying one-man-processing or re-distribution of the work elements to just below the takt time?

トヨタ生産方式とは？
What is TPS?

トヨタ生産方式とは？

トヨタ生産方式とは、企業の競争力を高めるための理念と手法のフレームワークです。

The Toyota Production System is a framework of concepts and methods to enhance corporate vitality.

トヨタ生産方式が目指すもの

トヨタ生産方式とは、徹底したムダ廃除を通してより良い品質、より低いコスト、より短いリードタイムを実現するために、トヨタ自動車で創案され、工夫されてきた生産方式です。

TPS is the production system developed by Toyota Motor Corporation to provide the best quality, the lowest cost, and the shortest lead time through the elimination of waste.

トヨタ生産方式とは考え方であり、その一方で、先人の努力の結集としての手法体系でもあるために、これを一言で表現するのはなかなか難しいことです。また、トヨタ生産方式にはこれで完成という形はなく、それゆえ今日までの手法体系をして「トヨタ生産方式とは」と語ることは危険でもあります。とはいうものの、海外工場で改善を始めるに当たって、簡潔に説明しなくてはならないというケースは多いはず。そのような場面での基本的な表現を紹介します。

◇トヨタ生産方式の2本柱

トヨタ生産方式の2本柱は、にんべんのついた自働化とジャスト・イン・タイムです。そのイメージは、右ページの図のような「家」の形で表現されます。

The two pillars of TPS are "jidoka" and "just-in-time". The basic image of TPS is often illustrated with the "house" shown here.

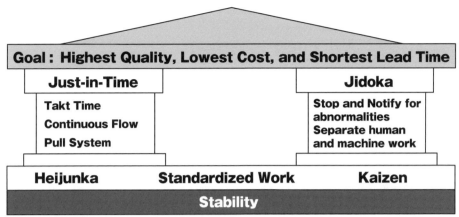

Basic Image of the Toyota Production System : the TPS House

◇トヨタ生産方式の誕生と大野耐一氏

豊田喜一郎氏が国産乗用車の開発を目指してトヨタ自動車工業（自工）を設立したのは1937年のことです。6年後、豊田紡織の自工への合併に伴い大野耐一氏（1912-1990）が自工へ転籍。戦後、喜一郎氏は「3年でアメリカに追いつけ！」という高い目標を掲げて会社の再生を率いました。

トヨタ生産方式が生まれたのは第二次世界大戦後の1947年のことでした。大野耐一氏がトヨタの機械工場で「手待ちのムダ」を発見したのです。

TPS was essentially born in 1947 in the post-WWII period. Mr. Taiichi Ohno identified "the waste of waiting" at the machine shop at Toyota.

大野氏は後にトヨタ自動車工業の副社長となりますが、トヨタ生産方式が今日見るような統合的なシステムとして築かれていく過程で、最も大きく貢献した人物です。

Mr. Ohno—who later became an executive vice president at Toyota—was the man who did the most to structure TPS as an integrated framework.

◇２人の偉人と２本柱のルーツ

自働化とジャスト・イン・タイムのルーツは、ともに第二次大戦前にあります。それは、大正年間に佐吉翁が完成させた自動織機と、自動車をムダなく開発・生産しようという喜一郎氏の創業の信念でした。

トヨタグループの社祖である豊田佐吉翁（1867-1930）は、20世紀初頭に自働化のコンセプトを具現化しました。

Mr. Sakichi Toyoda (1867-1930), founder of the Toyota Group, invented the concept of jidoka in the early 20th Century.

佐吉翁の子息であり、トヨタ自動車の創業者・豊田喜一郎氏（1894-1952）は、1930年代にジャスト・イン・タイムの概念を創案しました。

Mr. Kiichiro Toyoda (1894-1952), son of Sakichi and founder of Toyota automobile business developed the concept of just-in-time in the 1930's.

佐吉翁とにんべんのついた自働化

大正年間に豊田佐吉翁が完成させた自動織機には、**糸が切れたら自動的に停止する機構**がついていました。品質は劇的に改善され、機械の見張り番から作業者を解放して、多台持ちを可能にしました。後に、異常が発生したら自動停止するとともに、その異常を知らせるように設備を設計するという考え方は「にんべんのついた自働化」と呼ばれ、**トヨタのあらゆる設備、あらゆるライン、あらゆる仕事のやり方にとって不可欠なものになりました。**

―佐吉翁の自動織機 　　　　―Sakichi's automatic loom
―糸が切れたら自動停止　　　―It would stop automatically
　　　　　　　　　　　　　　　whenever a thread broke.

―品質と生産性を劇的に改善　―It enabled great improvement
　　　　　　　　　　　　　　　in quality and productivity.

喜一郎氏とジャスト・イン・タイム

豊田喜一郎氏はフォードシステムを研究し、日本にこれを適用すべく、ジャスト・イン・タイムを提唱しました。1938年のことです。

―ジャスト・イン・タイムを提唱　―Kiichiro declared just-in-time
　　　　　　　　　　　　　　　　　as company policy in 1938.

生産革新推進室――Lean Promotion Office――

いわゆる「生産革新推進室」の役割は重要です。推進室の役割を整理しましょう。呼び名は会社によってさまざまですが、ここでは、一般的に使われている"Lean Promotion Office"を使って紹介します。

推進室とは改革を推進するためのチームであり、その役割は次のようなものです。

A Lean Promotion Office is a team to support a lean transformation. This team provides managers assistance with :

・改善計画の立案
・手法の教育・訓練
・モデル工場をつくる
・実践会の企画・運営
・進捗チェックと推進計画の見直し

・Making kaizen plans.
・Training in lean methods.
・Developing model production sites.
・Conducting kaizen workshops.
・Measuring progress and revising plans.

Single machine Handling
1台持ち（単能工）

Multi-machine Handling
多台持ち（単能工）

Multi-process Handling
多工程持ち（多能工）

Let's talk　　自働化と多台持ち、多工程持ち

A： 大野さんが初めて手待ちのムダを発見したとき、多台持ちにしたと聞くけれど、大野さんはどうやって多台持ちを思いついたの？

B： 大野さんは豊田紡織での経験から、自働化の機構があれば、1人の作業者が何十台もの織機を持てることを知っていたんだ。

A： だから、機械の見張りはムダだと気づくことができたのね！　次に、大野さんが気づいたのがつくり過ぎのムダですね。どうしてつくり過ぎがムダだと気づくことができたのかしら？

B： 戦後、大野さんはできるだけ早くアメリカの生産性に追いつき、追い抜きたいという目標を持っていた。国内市場は小さく、戦争で傷ついた日本経済にはお金もなかった。だから、アメリカの大量生産とは違う方法を見つけるしかなかったんだよ。

A： とうとう、大野さんはロットを小さくして、段取り替えを速やかにすることでつくり過ぎを抑え、結果として安くつくることができると証明したのですね。

A： I have heard that Mr. Ohno tried multi-machine handling when he identified the waste of waiting for the first time. How did he get that idea?

B： From his experience at Toyoda Boshoku, he had known that a jidoka device had enabled a single operator to handle dozens of looms.

A： So he could find the waste of monitoring machines! Next, Mr. Ohno found the waste of overproduction. Why was he able to identify it as waste?

B： In the post-WWII period, Mr. Ohno had the objective to outstrip the productivity in the US as soon as possible. The domestic market was small and the war-torn Japanese economy was starved for capital. So Toyota had to find some new way that was different from mass production in the US.

A： Eventually, Mr. Ohno proved that producing smaller batches with quick changeovers actually resulted in cost savings while preventing overproduction.

TPSが人と設備に求めるもの
TPS puts People and Machines together!

👦 人も設備も変わらなければ！

トヨタ生産方式は、これに関わるすべての人と設備に、変革を求めるものです。

なめらかな流れを実現するためには、お客様の要求に合うように、すべての従業員・管理職、サプライヤー、そして設備もすべて変わらなくてはなりません。

Creating a smooth stream requires that every employee, every manager, every supplier, and every machine will change, to meet the requirements of the customers.

◇見かけの能率と真の能率

では、人と設備は、どのように変わるべきなのでしょうか？そのヒントとなるのが、「見かけの能率と真の能率」「個々の能率と全体の効率」という考え方です。故・大野耐一氏は、見かけの能率と真の能率を混同してはいけない、と厳しく指摘しました。

見かけの能率‥‥‥‥‥‥‥‥‥‥‥‥‥‥‥‥
売れ行きに関係なく、現状の人や設備のまま生産量を増やすこと。これは、単なる計算上の能率向上に過ぎない。

真の能率‥‥‥‥‥‥‥‥‥‥‥‥‥‥‥‥‥‥
売れる数量だけを、最少限の人と設備で生産し、能率を上げる方法。限量経営の考え方からきており、真の原価低減に結びつく。

Apparent Efficiency

Apparent Efficiency means increasing production output with no change in the number of operators or equipment, without being tied to sales or market demands. It is an improvement mathematically only.

True Efficiency

True Efficiency means producing the number of parts or products that can be sold while utilizing the minimum number of operators and equipment possible. True Efficiency is the result of "Genryou Management" and results in true cost reduction.

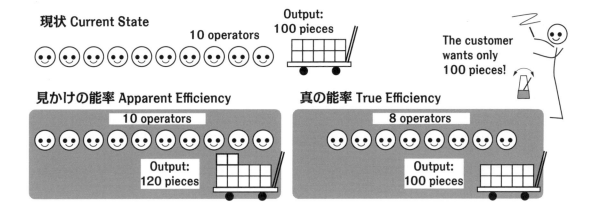

◇個々の能率と全体の効率

また大野氏は、個々の能率だけを追求し過ぎるとつくり過ぎを生み、全体の効率を損なう場合があることに注意しなくてはならない、と言っています。

個々の能率 · **Local Efficiency**

前後の工程やお客様とは無関係に、個々の工程の能率を追求すること。

Local Efficiency means boosting the efficiency at a certain line, process or machine, completely separated from previous or following processes or customers.

全体の効率 · **Total Productivity**

個々の工程における見かけの能率ではなく、流れの全域にわたって真の能率を向上させて、企業全体の生産性を高めること。

Total Productivity means seeking to improve not apparent efficiency at one local point, but true efficiency through the entire production flow that results in greater overall company productivity. (Sometimes called "System Efficiency")

◇多能工化と設備改善で流れ化を

多能工化 · **Multi-Skilled Operator**

流れをつくり、真の能率を向上させるためには、作業者は、いろいろな機械の操作や、多種の作業を担当できなくてはなりません。

In order to create continuous flow and improve true efficiency, an operator must be able to perform many different jobs and to operate diverse types of machines.

設備改善 · **Right-sized Equipment**

流れの中で設備を活かすには、タクトタイムに合った速度で正しく動作し、大き過ぎず、かつ安価という新しいタイプの設備が必要です。これを、私たちは "Right-sized" と呼んでいます。

In order to place equipment in the production flow, we need equipment which runs at the rate to match takt time, is more inexpensive and is not too large. We call this "Right-sized" equipment.

設備改善の着眼点

TPSが求める設備とはどのようなものか、着眼点を整理しましょう。ここでは、新規投資について説明します。

設備改善の着眼点 ·················	**"Right-sized"tools and equipment**
①付加価値を生む部分に注目する ········	①Focus on the actual value-creating part
機械の中の、付加価値を生まないムダな動きや搬送をできるだけ小さくします。	Motion and conveyance in the machine that does not create value should be minimized.
②必要な能力（不良ゼロ、タクトタイム） ········	②Capability to meet customer requirements
不良をつくらず、想定されるタクトタイムで動くことが求められますが、タクトタイム以上に速く動く必要はありません。	Equipment must be capable to run at the rate of estimated takt time while making no defects. But it does not need to run more quickly than takt time.
③メンテナンスしやすい ·················	③Easy to Maintain
④可動率を高く ····················	④High Operational Availability
動くべきときには正しく動かなくてはなりません。	It must be available whenever needed to run.
⑤素早い段取り替えが可能 ·············	⑤Easy to Changeover Quickly
⑥移設が簡単 ·····················	⑥Easy to Move
⑦より小さく、より安く ·················	⑦Smaller and lower cost

高速、多機能、高価、大型
-too fast
-too many functions
-too expensive
-too large

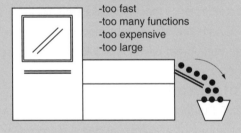

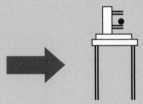

付加価値を生む部分に着目して設備を改善する。
Redesign the machine with focus on the part which creates value.

スキル管理板をつくろう―Let's make a Skills Training Matrix Board!―

管理者は、作業者に対する教育訓練プログラムを日常的に実施する必要があります。スキル管理板は、訓練計画の基本をなすものです。

Managers should always provide training for operators. The Skills Training Matrix Board is the basis of the training plan.

Skills Training Matrix	◐ Can do generally ● Certified ◑ Can do well ● Can do training										Factory name: Made By:	Foreman: Date:
	Processes										Current Date	Target Date
#	Operator	Cut	Bend	Grind	Weld	Test	Repair	Assem	M.Test	E.Test	Shipping		
1	Operator A	◐	◐	◐	◔	◑	◑	○	◔	○	○		
2	Operator B	◔	◑	◑	◑	◑	◑	○	○	○	○		
3	Operator C	○	○	○	○	○	●	○	●	●	●		
	...												

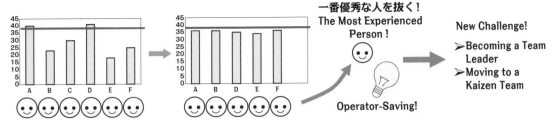

改善の成果を分かち合おう！　**Improvements Leads to Shared Success.**

一番優秀な人を抜く！
The Most Experienced Person !

New Challenge!
➢ Becoming a Team Leader
➢ Moving to a Kaizen Team

Operator-Saving!

Let's talk　　改善の成果を分かち合う

A： 今までの改善で、ラインから作業者を抜くことができました。でも、その結果が失業だとしたら、これ以上は、誰だって協力しようとは思えないですよね？

A： We have freed up some operators through kaizen. But surely nobody will be willing to support kaizen if it results in loss of employment.

B： よい指摘です。どのような仕事であれ、永遠に変わらぬままということはあり得ませんが、可能な限り雇用を守るのは経営の責務です。

B： Good point! While no task stays the same forever, management should try to provide secure employment as long as possible.

A： そうあってほしいわ。雇用を脅かされる心配がないのなら、誰でもアイデアを出したり、それを実現したりしたいと、強く願っているはずよ。

A： We all hope so. I think that people are usually eager to give and realize their ideas for more kaizen if it doesn't threaten job security.

B： そうだね。抜いた作業者について、きちんとした計画をマネジメントは持つべきです。別の意義ある仕事についてもらわなくては。

B： I think so, too. Therefore, management needs to have a reliable plan for them once they are freed from their current work. They need to go to other meaningful work.

A： チームリーダーになる訓練はどうかしら。

A： How about training to become a team leader?

B： その通り。だから、ラインから人を抜くときは、ナンバーワンの熟練者を選んで、その人に新たな挑戦をしてもらう。リーダーになるとか、推進室に移ってもらうとか。

B： Yes. So, when you get one operator-saving, you take the most experienced operator and set him or her to new challenges, such as being a leader, or moving to the Lean Promotion Team.

A： それなら、改善の目的が、単に人数を減らすことではなくて、現場をよりよくすることや、人の能力を引き出すことにあるんだ、ということが私たちにもよくわかるわ。

A： That is a nice way for us to recognize that the purpose of kaizen is to make processes better and to develop people's abilities, not to simply reduce the number of operators.

Chapter

2

ジャスト・イン・タイム
Just-in-Time with Flow, Pull and Heijunka

ジャスト・イン・タイム
What is Just-in-Time?

ジャスト・イン・タイムとは？

ジャスト・イン・タイムとは、必要なものを、必要なときに、必要なだけつくり、提供する生産システムのことです。

Just-in-time means a system of production that makes and delivers what is needed, just when it is needed, and just in the amount needed.

ジャスト・イン・タイムが目指すもの

それでは、「必要」とはどんな意味なのでしょうか。トヨタ生産方式では、お客様を起点に考えます。

お客様は、より良い製品を、より安く、できるだけ早く欲しいと考えます。

Customers want the best possible products at the lowest possible prices. And they want them as soon as possible.

そして、お客様の満足と生産サイドの効率化をともに達成しようとするのです。

ジャスト・イン・タイムは、徹底したムダ廃除を通して、より良い品質のものを、より低いコスト、より少ない資源、より短いリードタイムで製造し、お客様に提供することを目指したものです。

Just-in-time aims for the total elimination of all waste to achieve the best possible quality, the lowest possible cost and use of resources, and the shortest possible production and delivery lead times.

◇ジャスト・イン・タイムの３つの要素

ジャスト・イン・タイムは平準化を大前提とし、3つの要素で支えられます。タクトタイム、流れ化、後工程引き取りです。

Just-in-time relies on heijunka as a foundation and is comprised of three elements: takt time, continuous flow and pull system.

Just-in-Time relies on Heijunka and is comprised of three elements.

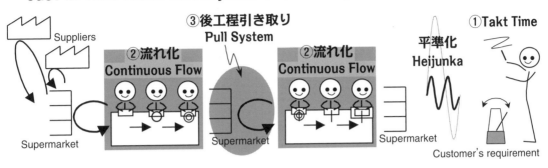

◇タクトタイムと流れ化、後工程引き取り

> タクトタイムと流れ化、後工程引き取りは、ジャスト・イン・タイムを支える要素ですが、この3つは、密接につながり合って初めて成果として結実するものです。

タクトタイムとは、お客様の要求に合うように、売れに合わせて、部品1個、製品1個をどのくらいの速さでつくればよいかを示すものです。

Takt time is how often you should produce one part or product to meet customer requirements based on the rate of sales.

流れ化とは、タクトタイムに合わせて、1度に1個ずつ、1つの工程から次の工程へと停滞なく（ほかのいろいろなムダもなく）、すいすいと流れていく1個流しを意味します。

Continuous flow means producing and moving one item at a time to match takt time, with each item passed immediately from one process step to the next without stagnation (or any other waste) in between.

トヨタ生産方式の中核をなす考え方は、売れに合わせて、すべての工程を加工の順番に並べて1本のスムーズな流れをつくること、です。

A core concept of TPS is arranging all the processes in the production sequence in a single, smooth flow based on the rate of sales.

> しかし、すべての工程を1個流しでつなぐことは、最初はなかなか難しいものです。上流工程へ目を向けると、クリーンルーム内でなければ加工できない、高額な高速設備で加工している、また、ほかの製品群との共用で専用化は不可能、というようなケースが多いものです。これらすべてをはじめから1個流しでつなぐことは、現実的とは言えません。

最初は、流れ化と後工程引き取りの組合せから始めるのがよいでしょう。そして、工程の安定化や段取り改善、インライン設備の開発などに合わせて、流れ化の範囲を広げていくのです。

A good approach can be to begin with a combination of continuous flow and pull system. Then extend the range of continuous flow as reliability is improved, changeover times are reduced, and in-line equipment is developed.

ワンポイントレッスン

タクトタイムを計算する

タクトタイム

$$= \frac{\text{シフト当たりの定時稼働時間}}{\text{シフト当たりの要求数量}}$$

例：27,000秒÷455個＝59秒

タクトタイムに合わせてつくることは単純と感じられるかもしれませんが、努力なしには成り立ちません。
・問題に対して素早く（タクト内で）対応する
・想定外のダウンの原因をなくす
・段取り時間を短縮する

Takt Time

$$= \frac{\text{available working time per shift}}{\text{customer demand rate per shift}}$$

example: 27,000sec. ÷ 455pieces ＝ 59sec.

Producing to takt time sounds simple, but is the result of concentrated efforts to:
・provide fast response (within takt time) to problems
・eliminate causes of unplanned downtime
・reduce changeover time

役立つ豆知識

米国で再発見されたモノと情報の流れ図—Value-Stream Mapping—

点の改善（個々の工程の作業改善や設備改善）は重要です。しかし、ムダの真因を見つけ、全体を改善するためには（＝線の改善）、工場全体、さらには顧客から商品物流、サプライヤーまでも含めた全体を視野に入れて、改善計画を立てることが欠かせません。

そこで役立つのが「モノと情報の流れ図」（Value-Stream Mapping＝VSM）なのですが、日本ではあまり知られていません。この図が持つ力を再発見したのは、アメリカ人のJohn Shook氏（本書の協力者）とMike Rother氏です。トヨタでは、重要な手法として名づけられることもなく、昔から自然に使われていたようです。

点の改善は不可欠ですが、ムダの真因を見つけて、全体を改善する実行計画を立案し、実現するためには、VSMがとても役立ちます。設計図なしに家を建てることを想像してみてください。

Process kaizen is critical. However, VSM is useful to identify the sources of waste and to plan and realize total system kaizen. Imagine trying to build a house without a blueprint!

Future-State Map（将来）

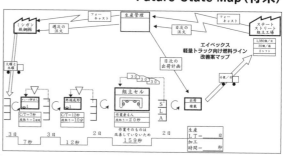

Current-State Map（現状）

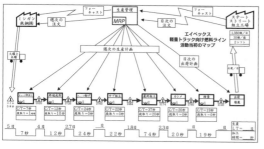

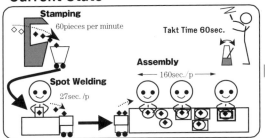

Current State

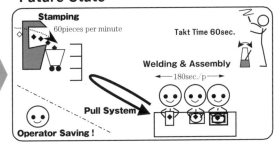

Future State

Let's talk 流れ化で直接つなぐvs.引き取りでつなぐ

A： ここが私たちの現場です。最初の工程はプレス、次がスポット溶接、最後が組立です。

B： タクトタイムは何秒ですか？ それから、各工程では、何秒かかっていますか？

A： タクトタイムは60秒。組立は全部で160秒、溶接は27秒です。プレスは自動加工で、1分間に60個。プレスはこの製品だけの専用ではありません。

B： 溶接と組立で187秒、187秒をタクトタイム60で割ると3.12。まずは、溶接から組立までを流れ化し、4人ではなく、3人編成とするべきです。

A： すごいわ！ 1人抜くことができますね！プレスはどうしましょう？

B： 今すぐにプレスを流れ化するのは、現実的ではありません。プレスのサイクルは高速過ぎるし、ほかの製品のために段取り替えも必要です。ですから、プレス設備を改善するまでの間は、後工程引き取りを採用しなければなりません。

A： Here is our workplace. The first process is stamping, then spot-welding, and the final process is assembly.

B： What is your takt time? And, how many seconds does it take for each process?

A： Takt time is 60 seconds. Total work time is 160 seconds per piece at assembly, and 27 seconds at welding. Stamping automatically produces 60 pieces per minute. Stamping is not dedicated for this product.

B： Total work time is 187 seconds for welding and assembly. Then we get 3.12 by dividing 187 seconds by takt time 60. So we should first connect welding to assembly as a continuous flow and assign three operators, not four.

A： Great! We can get one operator-saving! What should we do about stamping?

B： Incorporating stamping into a continuous flow right now is not practical. Its cycle is too quick for this product and it changes over for other products. So we should use a pull system until the stamping machine will be right-sized.

流れ化
What is Continuous Flow?

🙂 流れ化とは？

流れ化とは、タクトタイムに合わせて、可能な限り工程順につないだ１本の流れに沿って、１度に１つずつ（あるいは小さな一定量ずつ）、つくり、運ぶことです。各工程では、次の工程が求める分だけをつくります。

Continuous flow means producing and moving one item at a time (or a small and consistent batch) through a series of processing steps as continuously as possible, to match takt time, with each step making just what is required by the next step.

１個流しの流れ化を"Continuous Flow"と呼び、一般的な流れについて言及するときは単に"Flow"と呼んで、使い分けることによって、改善への理解が深まるはずです。

◇フォード式流れ生産と、流れ化

流れ生産は、ヘンリー・フォード氏が、1913年にミシガン州ハイランドパークの工場で実現した世界初の画期的な生産システムでした。下記のような一連の技術革新によって、製品が完成するまでに必要な時間と人の作業とを、大幅に削減したのです。今日の産業社会に大きな影響を与えました。

フォード式流れ生産における技術革新 ……………

- ●部品に一定の互換性を持たせ、ライン上の各作業のサイクルタイムのばらつきをなくす。

- ●ライン化それ自体が革新的で画期的。
- ●部品の加工方法を見直し、機械を加工順に並べて、機械から機械へ、素早く滑らかに流す。

- ●最終組立ラインの部品所要に合わせて部品を加工するように、生産管理システムを整備する。

The Innovations of the Ford System

- ●Consistently interchangeable parts so that cycle times could be stable for every job along an extended line.
- ●The assembly line itself.
- ●The reconfiguration of parts fabrication tasks so that machines were lined up in process sequence with parts flowing quickly and smoothly from machine to machine.
- ●A production control system ensuring that the rate of parts fabrication matched the consumption rate of parts in final assembly.

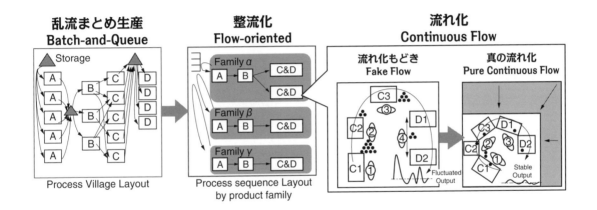

乱流まとめ生産 Batch-and-Queue	整流化 Flow-oriented	流れ化 Continuous Flow
Storage Process Village Layout	Family α Family β Family γ Process sequence Layout by product family	流れ化もどき Fake Flow Fluctuated Output 真の流れ化 Pure Continuous Flow Stable Output

トヨタ生産方式は、フォード式から多くを学んでいます。「流れ化」は、戦後のトヨタが資金難を克服するため、また、小さかった国内市場に合わせるため、フォード式をさらに進化させたものと言えるでしょう。

1950年代のトヨタは、小さなロットで、より安く、より速く、車をつくる方法を開発するほかなかったのです。	Toyota in the 1950's had to develop some new method to produce cars more quickly in smaller lots at lower cost.

◇単なる「流れ」から、流れ化へ

素材から製品を完成するまで、**最も速い方法は流れ化**なのに、歴史的に、私たちは大量生産の考え方に基づいて、**分業型レイアウト**を採ってきました。人間は、直感的に、まとめることを好むのかもしれません。	Even though the fastest way to translate raw material into finished products is continuous flow, historically we have adopted process village layout based on the concept of mass production. The human mind may like batches intuitively!

まとめ生産から流れ生産に変えるには、次のようなステップで進めます。

流れ化実現へのステップ ··················	**The Road to Continuous Flow**
①製品ごとの工程経路を分析し製品群を定義する。	①Defining the product families through analyzing paths for each item.
②可能な限り、すべての工程を加工順に並べる。	②Relocating process steps, wherever possible, into process sequences for product families.
③もう一度、「流れ化の目で」見て改善する。 ・タクトタイムと出来高のバラツキ ・工程間の仕掛品の停滞 ・動作のムダ	③Looking again at the flow with "eyes for continuous flow" to realize pure continuous flow. −Fluctuated output in discord with takt time −Small stagnation between steps −Waste of motion

ワンポイントレッスン

流れ化の着眼点

流れ化の着眼点を整理しましょう …………………… A Closer Look
…with Eyes for Continuous Flow

①出来高のバラツキ ……………………………………… ① Fluctuated Output

まず、**生産管理板**を見る（なければあなたがつ
くること）。どのような理由であれ、タクトタ
イムに対する出来高のばらつきは、大きな改善
可能性の存在を示す。

First, look at the Production Analysis Board (if
there is no Board, make one yourself!).
Whatever the cause, fluctuated output that is
slower or quicker than takt time is clear
evidence that line performance can be greatly
improved.

②工程間の停滞 ………………………………………… ② Stagnation between steps

工程間に停滞があるのなら、そこには必ず問題
がある。真因を突き止めなくてはならない。

Wherever there is stagnation between steps,
there are problems. You have to find the root
cause.

③人の動き ……………………………………………… ③ Operator's Motion

繰返しのサイクルから外れた動きはバッチ作業
の可能性大。手待ちは**分業**によって生じる場合
が多い。動作のムダは**部品の置き方**の悪さを示
す。

Operators leaving their regular work often
means they are working in batches rather than
one-piece flow. Waiting is often caused by
decoupled operations. Waste of motion
indicates problems of parts presentation.

④レイアウト …………………………………………… ④ Layout

1人作業の1個流しレイアウトと比較すること
で、現状のレイアウト上の問題を顕在化させる
ことができる。

Comparing the current layout with one-piece
layout for one operator helps you to reveal
problems in the current layout.

役立つ豆知識

生産管理板は、必須の改善ツール―Production Analysis Board is an invaluable tool!―

生産管理板とは、時間単位に
出来高の計画と実績を表示し
た掲示板です。セル（または
ライン）の出口に、必ず設置
しなければなりません。

Production Analysis Board is a display
that should be located at the exit of the
cell or line, to show actual performance
compared with planned performance
on an hourly basis.

Production Analysis Board

TaktTimeを必ず書く

Remember breaks

Cell/Line : **Fuel Line Cell**		Team Leader : **Mary Smith**			
Quantity Required : **690p**		TaktTime : **40sec**			
Time	Hourly		Cumulative		Problems/Causes	Sign-off
	Plan/Actual		Plan/Actual			
06:00～07:00	90/90		90/90			
07:00～08:00	90/88		180/178		Tester failure	
08:00～09:10	90/90		270/268			
09:10～10:10	90/85		360/353		Tester failure	
10:10～11:10	90/90		450/443			
11:40～12:40	90/90		540/533			
12:40～13:40	90/86		630/619		Bad Parts (valves)	
13:50～14:30	60/60		690/679			
O.T.	11/11		690/690		(8 minutes)	

Supervisor
signs hourly

Area Manager
signs at lunch
and end of shift

出来高のバラツキの背後には、何ら
かの問題が存在する！
Fluctuated output is the evidence of
some hidden problems!

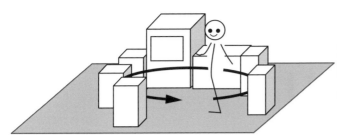

1人完結なら、どんなレイアウト？

How can the physical processes be laid out so one operator can make one piece as efficiently as possible?

Let's talk

U字型の意味

A： 先週は、ブライト工業の工場を見学するチャンスがあって、いろいろなU字セルをたくさん見ました。U字には、どんな意味があるの？

B： ライン設計にあたって、1人完結で最初から最後までつくると仮定して、一筆書きができるように、設備、作業台、部品供給治具を配置してみる。実際にはそういう運用をしないとしても、ね。

A： 確かに、離れ小島も避けられる、工程間の停滞も抑えられる、歩行のムダもないし、動作線上の障害物もない、作業者は付加価値を生まない作業から開放される…、というようなラインを、自動的に設計できるわ。だから、多くのセルが、おのずと狭いU字型になるのですね。

B： もちろん、ラインのレイアウトは、製品、設備、部品供給方法などに影響されるものです。ですから、実際には、さまざまな形のラインが可能です。

A： Last week, I had the chance to do a plant walk-through at Bright Industries and saw many various U-shape cells. What advantages does the U-shape provide?

B： When you design the line, you arrange the machines, workstations and parts presentation devices in a series of processing steps, as if only one operator makes the product from beginning to end, even if you will never run the line with one operator.

A： In this way, I can automatically design a line that avoids isolated islands, minimizes inventory accumulation between steps, eliminates excessive walking, removes obstacles on the walking paths and frees the operator from non-value-creating work. So, many cells naturally end up in a tight U-shape.

B： Of course, the line layout is often affected by the products, the equipment and parts presentation issues so various different shapes are possible.

後工程引き取り

Do Not Push Anything, Anywhere, at Any Time.

押し込みはいけない

TPS用語の多くと同じように、「後工程引き取り」もまた、基本的な考え方としての「引き取り」を表す場合と、手法やルールを説明する場合の違いを意識して表現を使い分けることにより、英語圏の人々にさらに理解を深めてもらうことができるようです。

考え方としての「後工程引き取り」

引き取りとは、押し込みの反対で、お客様である後工程から要求があるまでは、いつでも、どこでも、製品や部品やサービスをつくったり、渡したりしてはいけない、という意味です。押し込みは、つくり過ぎのムダをつくり出してしまいます。

Pull Concept

Pull is the opposite of Push. It means that nobody upstream should produce or deliver products, parts or services, anywhere at any time, until the customer downstream requires it. Pushing things to the next process causes overproduction.

◇後工程引き取りとは

ジャスト・イン・タイムを支える引き取り

後工程引き取りは、ジャスト・イン・タイムを支える主要な3要素の3つ目です。3要素とは、タクトタイム、流れ化、そして後工程引き取りです。先の2つに加えて、後工程引き取りがきちんとできてくると、つくり過ぎを抑え、すべてのプロセスの棚卸しを低減することができるのです。

Pull System to support Just-in-Time

Pull system is the third of three major elements that compose just-in-time（along with takt time and continuous flow）. A well-devised pull system, in addition to the other two elements, can prevent overproduction and reduce the inventory in every process.

後工程の人が引く

後工程引き取りでは、後工程が前工程に、情報を渡します。このとき、いわゆる「かんばん」がよく使われます。

Starting from the customer downstream

In a pull system, downstream operations provides information to upstream operations, often via a kanban card.

Pushing things downstream causes Overproduction!

Overproduction
つくり過ぎ！

Here you go!
お待たせしましたぁ！

I don't need all this!
こんなに要らないってば！

かんばんは目で見る管理の道具 ·············

引き取り方式を実現するためには、前工程に対して生産の指示を与えたり、みずすましに対して引き取りの指示を出したりするための、誰にでもわかるような、何らかの道具が必要です。かんばんは、このような伝達手段の中で、最もよく知られ、また最も一般的なものです。

Kanban is a visual tool to run a Pull System.

In a pull system, we need some sort of signaling device that give instructions to upstream suppliers for production, or to the material handlers for withdrawal. Kanban cards are the best-known and most common of these signaling devices.

◇最終製品をどうつくる？　スーパーマーケットor受注生産

あなたが現在取り組んでいるテーマが上流工程の改善だとしても、それを全体の改善へとつなげるためには、最終製品をどのようにつくるのかということが、まず決まっていなければなりません。どこの改善であれ、あらゆる改善は、お客様に最も近い最下流（出荷場ないし最終組立ライン）を起点とし、「後工程はお客様」というアナロジーによって上流工程へと展開すべきなのです。

スーパーマーケット方式（在庫を持つ） ···············

最も基本的、共通的な方式です。スーパーマーケットは、単なる製品の置き場ではなく、お客様が製品を引き取ったら、その分だけ補充し、在庫を一定の量に保つ機能を持ちます。「Aタイプのプル」とも言います。

Supermarket Pull System

The Supermarket system is the most basic and most common type of pull system. A supermarket is not only a storage place, but creates pull by requiring replenishment or by plugging gaps created in the finished goods store when the customer withdraws product. Supermarket Pull is sometimes referred to as "A-Type Pull".

受注生産（在庫を持たない） ···············

「Bタイプのプル」とも言います。顧客からの注文頻度が低く、顧客が望むリードタイムが、ペースメーカー工程から出荷までのリードタイムよりも長いときに使う方法です。Aタイプよりも棚卸しを低く抑えることができますが、安定した流れと短いリードタイムが必須です。

Building directly to shipping

Building directly to shipping is part of what is sometimes referred to as "B-Type Pull", often used when order frequency is low and customer lead-time is longer than your lead-time from pacemaker to delivery. It can keep the inventory at lower levels than A-Type, but the reliability of your stream and shorter lead-time are crucial!

運搬が流れをつくる

トヨタ生産方式では、運搬は、流れにリズムを与える重要な機能とされています。

運搬は、単にモノを運ぶだけのものではありません。運搬それ自体が生産指示となり、また異常を見つける働きをすることが求められます。

Conveyance does much more than just deliver things. Conveyance itself should become production instruction, and perform as a checker on abnormalities in workplaces.

定量運搬と定時運搬

みずすましによる少量定時多頻度運搬を採用する工場が増えています。しかし、故・大野耐一氏が、戦後間もないトヨタの機械工場で引き取りを始めたときには、文字通り「後工程の人が、要るときに、要るものを、要るだけ、前工程へ取りに行く」という定量不定期運搬であったことを忘れてはいけないでしょう。運搬を設計するときは、まず、あなた自身が引き取りに行くことから始めるべきです。

Discussion Point	How to Convey	
	Fixed-Quantity, Unfixed-Time	Fixed-Time, Unfixed-Quantity
Inventory	Supplier must adapt to variable times	Supplier must adapt to variable quantities
Withdrawal time	Variable	Fixed
Quantity withdrawn	Fixed	Variable
Usage	✓ Processes connected as a virtual flow ✓ Short conveyance distances ✓ Large lots upstream	✓ Disconnected processes ✓ Job Shop Layout ✓ Long-distance conveyance

 役立つ豆知識

スーパーマーケットのルーツはアメリカ

アメリカにはスーパーマーケットというものがあると知った大野耐一氏は、その考えを製造に活かして、1953年に初めて機械工場で「スーパーマーケット」をつくり、引き取りを始めました。やがて1956年に大野氏は米国を訪れますが、数々の大きな工場よりもスーパーマーケットが最も印象深かったと後に回顧しています。

Mr. Taiichi Ohno heard about supermarkets in the US in the middle of the 1940s and tried to apply its idea to the production line. In 1953, Mr. Ohno set up the first supermarket in Toyota's machine shop and began pull production. In 1956, he visited the US. He reflected later that the (US) supermarkets he visited at that time were more impressive for him than the big American factories he visited then.

Locate your supermarket as close as possible to the supplying process!
スーパーマーケットは、つくった工程のすぐ近くに置くべし

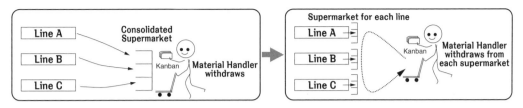

Let's talk　　スーパーマーケットをつくる

A： 先週、実践会でサブアセンブリ工程のスーパーマーケットをつくりました。アドバイスをお願いします。

A： Last week, we held a kaizen session and made a supermarket at the subassembly line. Would you please give us some advice to improve it?

B： 固定ロケーションにして、在庫の最大量を決めたんだね。これはよいと思います。しかし、つくったところから、遠過ぎるね。

B： You took on fixed-location and determined the maximum quantity for each item, didn't you? It is the right way to make a supermarket. But it is too far from the lines.

A： 遠過ぎるのですね？　それはわかっているのですが、ラインは3本あります。スーパーマーケットはどこに置けばよいのでしょうか？

A： Too far? We know that, but we have three subassembly lines. Where should we place the supermarket?

B： それぞれのラインのすぐ近くに、1つずつスーパーマーケットをつくるんです。みずすましは各ラインから引き取ります。

B： You had better set up one supermarket very close to each line. The material handler will withdraw items from each supermarket.

A： みずすましの仕事が増えてしまいます。

A： It will cause extra work for the material handler.

B： スーパーマーケットの目的は、離れた工程間を流れでつなぐこと、問題を素早く見つけて対策を実行することにあります。みずすましに過重な負担を強いることを避けるのはよいとしても、みずすましの仕事を減らすこと自体が目的ではありません。

B： Our objective with supermarkets is to connect processes that are physically disconnected as a flow, and to identify and solve problems more quickly. It may be better to avoid severe burden on material handlers, but reducing material handler's work itself is not our main objective.

A： なるほど、ラインのすぐ近くに置けば、誰が不良をつくったのか、よくわかりますね。

A： Okay. I can see that locating supermarkets closer to each line will help us to identify which line makes defects.

モノの置き方
Placing Things to Eliminate Waste

😊 モノの置き方でムダを取る

現場で、モノをどのように置くかということは、きわめて重要です。モノとは、完成品、仕掛品、部品、材料、棚、作業台、椅子、トレー、梱包資材、さまざまな工具や図面などのこと。

流れの目をもって工場を歩けば、モノのほとんどが、付加価値を付けられるでもなく、単に置かれているだけだということに、すぐに気づくでしょう。停滞は、すべてムダなのです。
さらに、部品や治具の置き方が悪いと、動作のムダや、不良をつくるムダを引き起こしてしまいます。

ですから、モノを置くときは、ムダを取るように置くことが大切なのです。
- ムダが見える置き方
- 停滞をなくす置き方
- 動作のムダやミスをなくす置き方

How to place things in the workplace is crucial. "Things" here means finished goods, work-in-process, parts, materials, shelves, workstations, chairs, containers, packaging materials, various tools or documents, etc.

When you walk through your plant with "eyes of flow", you will find soon that most things are simply stagnant without value being added. Any stagnation is waste.

In addition, the wrong parts presentation or wrong tools presentation often cause the waste of motion and the waste of making defects.

So, you should place things to eliminate waste as below:
- Visible presentation
- Preventing stagnation
- Eliminating the waste of motion and defects.

◇5Sは改善の基本…整理・整頓・清掃・清潔・しつけ

英語圏でも、5Sを改善の基盤と考える企業が増えています。以下では、英語圏の "Five Ss" 表現のうち、原義に近いフレーズを選択して紹介します。

5Sとは ·· ◄── Five Ss(= 5S)

5Sとは、Sで始まる次の5つの用語からなる、一見すると簡単そうに見えるシステムのこと。5Sは、改善の基盤です。

5Ss is a deceptively simple system composed of five related terms beginning with an S sound as below. It is the foundation of Kaizen.

Set in order（整頓）〜a place for everything and everything in its place〜

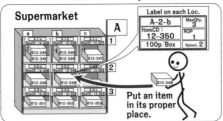

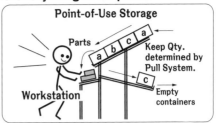

整理 ···································
要るモノと要らないモノを分けて、要らないモノ
を捨てる。

Sort out ["Seiri" in Japanese]
Separate needed from unneeded things and discard the unneeded.

整頓 ···································
要るモノだけを、使いやすいように、使う順に並べる。

Set in order ["Seiton" in Japanese]
Arrange items that are needed in a neat and easy-to-use manner and in sequence of using or consuming them.

清掃 ···································
きれいに掃除するのみならず、現場に何か異常がないか、点検することでもある。

Shine (and Inspect) ["Seiso" in Japanese]
The third S means not only sweeping up the work area, equipment and tools, but also inspection of something abnormal at the work area.

清潔 ···································
整理・整頓・清掃の３Sが保たれた状態。清潔とは、「汚すな」でもある。

Spic-and-Span ["Seiketsu" in Japanese]
The overall cleanliness and order that result from disciplined practice of the first three Ss. It means also "Don't litter the work area!"

しつけ（躾） ···················
４Sが身に付いていること。

Sustain ["Sitsuke" in Japanese]
Sustain the first four Ss. Sometimes referred to as "discipline".

◇キレイの基準を決める

整理・整頓の２Sについては、英語圏でも理解が深まっています。清掃を理解してもらうには、「キレイにする」とはどういうことなのかを、わかりやすく定義し、説明することが大切です。

「キレイにする」とは？ ···············
- 何を清掃するのか？
- どのように清掃するのか？
- 誰が清掃するのか？
- いつ、何回清掃するのか？
- どのくらいキレイにするのか？

We have to define our "Shine":
- What to clean?
- How to clean?
- Who will do the cleaning?
- How often to clean?
- How clean is clean?

ラインの中にモノを置く

ここでは、ムダをとるための部品や仕掛品、設備の置き方を説明します。

動作のムダをとる置き方 ·············

- 左右の手はそれぞれ同時並行。

- 一度に両手を使うなら、可能な限り、その動作を小さく。

- 軽作業なら、肩や上腕を動かさず、両手の範囲または前腕の範囲で。

- 作業者の動きは、滑らかに、流れるように。

- 作業者の前に最小限の半円を描き、その中で作業ができるように。ムリな姿勢をさせない。

- できるだけ、作業者の手を空ける。

For Economy of Motion

- Each hand-movement should be concurrent.

- Two-handed motion should be as compact as possible.

- Light work should be done with the hands and forearms, rather than the upper arms and shoulders.

- Motion should flow freely.

- Work should be done in a half-circle as small as possible in diameter in front of the operator. Maintain appropriate posture.

- Keep hands free as much as possible.

In the half-circle

ラインのレイアウトと設備の置き方 ·············

- 「売れ」に合わせて、あるいは作業者の身長に合わせて、配置を変えられるように。

- 部品は水平に搬送。垂直方向の動きは避ける。

- 重力を活用して部品を動かす（流れ棚など）。

- 人の動きと設備に合わせて、時計回りか、反時計回りかを決める。

Layout and Equipment

- Build flexibility into the layout to accommodate demand changes and taller or shorter operators.

- Move parts horizontally. Avoid vertical part movement.

- Use gravity to move parts (e. g., with sloping parts racks).

- Make a choice between clockwise or counter-clockwise to meet operators' motion and machines.

 役立つ豆知識

1個、2個と数えられる製品の改善では、入り数（収容数）とピッチを覚えておくと便利です。

Takt Time	×	Pack-Out Quantity		=	Pitch
60 sec./p	×		20p/container	=	20minutes

Let's Start from Shipping! 〜まずは出荷場から始めよう！〜

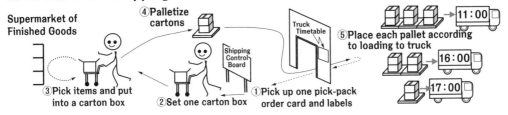

Let's talk まずは出荷場から始めよう！

A： 以前の実践会で、改善は出荷場から始めるべしと教えられましたよね。ここが出荷場です。

B： ピッキング作業者が製品を回転式自動倉庫から出して、梱包作業者が梱包しているんだね。出荷便は1日に何回？　ピッキング件数と出荷件数は日当たりで何件？

A： 3便で、11:00、16:00、17:00発です。ピッキング件数は約400件、出荷は100件です。梱包のタクトは、4分48秒です。

B： ピッキングから梱包、出荷まで、多工程持ちにすれば、4、5人ですべて出荷できると思うよ。今ここには、10人以上いるよね？

A： すごいわ！　すぐにやってみます。それでは、梱包した製品は、どう置けばよいの？

B： まず、トラックの時刻表を出口の壁に貼ること。それから、トラックごとに、今日の出荷オーダーを積載順に並べてリストをつくる。それを出荷管理板に貼るんだよ。

A： わかったわ！　そのリストの順に、梱包済みのモノを置くのですね。

A： In a previous kaizen session you told us to start from the shipping. This is our shipping area.

B： Packing operators pack products picked by pickers from carousels. How often does the truck leave per day? How many picking and shipping orders do you process per day?

A： The truck leaves three times every day, at 11am, 4pm and 5pm. We receive about 400 picking orders per day and about 100 shipping orders per day. So our packing takt time is 4 minutes and 48 seconds.

B： In that case, I think four or five operators will be able to process all orders through multi-process-handling from picking-packing to shipping. Over ten operators are working here now, aren't they?

A： Great! We'll try it from now. And then, how should we palletize packed products?

B： Put up a truck-timetable board first on the wall at the exit. Next, compile a list of today's shipping orders in sequence of palletizing and loading to each truck, and post the lists on a Shipping Control Board.

A： I got it! We'll place packed products according to those lists on the Board.

かんばん
What is Kanban ?

かんばんは、後工程引き取りの道具

日本国内では、かんばん＝トヨタ生産方式 ではない、ということが、広く理解されるようになりました。しかし海外では、トヨタ生産方式＝ジャスト・イン・タイム＝かんばん　と捉えている人がまだ多いように感じます。そこで、かんばんについて話すときは、常に、2本柱、タクトタイム、流れ化などの構造やセオリー、「かんばんは、後工程引き取りの道具、改善の道具」であること、等々を復習してから、かんばんそのものの話題に入るようにするのがよいでしょう。同じ話の繰返しはムダでは？とも思うでしょうが、私は、これについては、むしろ同じ話を何度でも繰り返すべきと考えます。

かんばんとは

かんばんとは、後工程引き取りにおいて、生産したり、引き取ったりしてよいという許可を与えたり、あるいは生産や引き取りをしなさいという指示を出したりする、ある種の信号のようなもの。引き取りとは、後工程からの要求に基づく運搬。

What is Kanban?

A kanban is a signaling device that gives authorization and instruction for the production or withdrawal of items in a pull system. "Withdrawal" means the conveyance called on by the downstream operation.

◇かんばんの具体像

かんばんカード（普通にかんばんと言えばこれ）········

カード型のかんばんは、後工程からの引きを伝える道具のうちで、最もよく知られ、また最もよく使われているものです。長方形の伝票のようなもので、ときに透明なビニールケースに入っています。一般的にかんばんに記載されるのは、

- 部品名と部品番号
- つくった人（ベンダーまたは社内の工程名）
- 収容数（入り数）
- ストアの所番地
- 使用する工程の所番地
- 引き取りのサイクル
  （バーコードが印刷されていることもある）

Kanban Card

Kanban cards are the best-known and most common example of pull signals. They often are slips of card stock, sometimes protected in clear vinyl envelopes, basically stating information such as below:

- Part name and part number
- Supplier or internal supplying process
- Pack-out quantity
- Storage address
- Consuming process address
- How often it is to be withdrawn
  (A bar code maybe printed on the card.)

生産指示かんばんと引き取りかんばん
Example of Production Kanban and Withdrawal Kanban

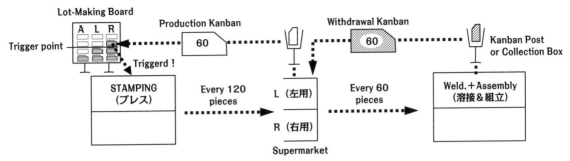

かんばんのいろいろな形
カードのほかにも、かんばんには、三角形の金属板や色付きボール、トレーそれ自体や電子的な信号などがあり、また、誤った指示を出すことなく、必要な情報だけを伝えることができるものなら何であれ、かんばんとして使うことができます。

Various Types of Kanban
Besides cards, kanban can be triangular metal plates, colored balls, containers themselves, electronic signals, or any other device that can convey the needed information while preventing the introduction of erroneous instructions.

◇生産指示かんばんと、引き取りかんばん

皆さんが働く国内の工場には、いろいろなかんばんがあることでしょう。しかし、海外では、初めのうちは、名称や形にはあまりこだわらず、「かんばんは、その機能から大きく２つに分類でき、それぞれにさまざまなかんばんがあり得る」と説明した方が、後の理解のためには役立ちます。

かんばんの２つの機能
その形状がどんなものであれ、かんばんは、製造において、２つの機能を持っています。つまり、製品や部品をつくりなさいと指示する機能と、運搬担当者に対して製品や部品を運びなさいと指示する機能です。前者を生産指示かんばん、後者を引き取りかんばんと呼びます。

Kanban have Two Functions.
Whatever the form, kanban have two functions in a production operation: They instruct processes to make products or parts, and they instruct material handlers to move products or parts. The former use is called production kanban; the latter use is termed withdrawal kanban.

生産指示かんばん
生産指示かんばんは、前工程に対して、後工程のために、どの製品（または部品）を、いくつつくりなさい、と伝えるものです。

Production Kanban
Production kanban (or "make cards") tell a supplying process the type and quantity of products (or parts) to make for a downstream process.

引き取りかんばん
引き取りかんばんは、製品（や部品）を後工程へ運んでよろしいという許可を与えます。工場内の「工程間引き取りかんばん」と、外部との間で使う「納入指示かんばん」の２種類があります。

Withdrawal Kanban
Withdrawal kanban (or "move cards") authorize the conveyance of products (or parts) to a downstream process. They often take two forms: internal (or interprocess) kanban and supplier kanban.

かんばんのルールは６つ——Six rules for using kanban effectively——

ほぼ定番表現になっているのですが、TPSの原典（複数）編纂の歴史的経緯と、英語圏におけるTPS研究進展の経緯から、微妙に異なる複数の英語版「６つのルール」が存在しています。皆さんの中には、海外工場の社員から、「どれが正しいのか？」と質問されて困惑した経験のある方もいらっしゃるのでは。順序や表現も大切ですが、まずは考え方をきちんと理解してもらうことを第一としましょう。ここでは、故・大野耐一氏の「トヨタ生産方式」をもとにした近年の英訳表現を紹介します。

①お客様である後工程は、かんばんが外れた分だけ、前工程から引き取る。

①Customer processes withdraw items in the precise amounts specified on the kanban. （近年では、必ずしも後工程の人が直接引き取りに行くとは限らないケースが増えてきたため、"withdraw items" に代えて、みずすましに指示を出すという意味で "order items" と表現する場合もあります）

②前工程は、かんばんが外れたものを、外れた分だけ、外れた順につくる。

②Supplier processes produce items in the precise amounts and sequence specified by the kanban.

③かんばんがないときは、つくらない、運ばない。

③No items are made or moved without a kanban.

④かんばんは、現物に必ず付けておく（または、モノには、必ずかんばんを付ける）。

④A kanban should always accompany each item. (Each item always has a kanban attached.)

⑤不良品を絶対に後工程へ送らない。

⑤Defects and incorrect amounts are never sent to the downstream process.

⑥かんばんの枚数を減らしていく。

⑥The number of kanban is reduced carefully to lower inventories and to reveal problems.

「おさわり２回」——何て言えばいいの？

「おさわり２回」、まさに言うは易く行うは難し、ですね。LEIの教材では、次の表現が紹介されています（"Making Materials Flow" より）。
Eliminate Triple Handling of Materials.
Material handlers should move the materials as directly as possible from the truck to the purchased-parts market, eliminating one or more unnecessary steps while improving quality and accuracy. …… Of course, in a perfect world, deliveries would go directly from the dock to the value-creating cells in one step. Unfortunately this is rarely possible……

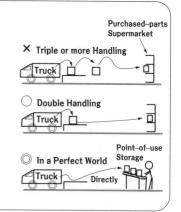

Purchased-parts Supermarket
× Triple or more Handling
Truck

○ Double Handling
Truck

Point-of-use Storage
◎ In a Perfect World
Truck   Directly

How often should the upstream supplying process fabricate parts?

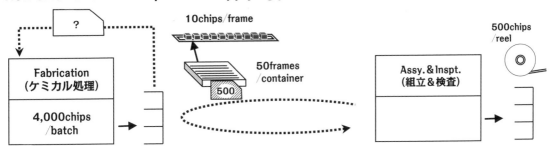

Let's talk 前工程へ引きを伝える

A： 最終組立は、前工程のスーパーマーケットから1トレーずつ引き取ります。1トレーには50フレーム、1フレームにはチップ10個が載っています。組立・検査の後、500チップずつ1本のテープリールに巻かれます。

B： 加工後のチップは何種類ですか？

A： チップは5種類です。でも、前工程の化学処理工程では、500チップずつつくっていたのでは、段取り時間が長過ぎて、必要な量をつくれません。チップの生産指示を、どのように出せばよいでしょう？

B： 500個ずつつくるのは、今はまだ現実的ではありませんね。ロット生産指示板を使って、4,000個ずつつくることにしようか。

A： スーパーマーケットの各トレーに生産指示かんばんを付けて、ロット生産指示板との間で回すのね。それでは、ロット生産指示板の発注点は、いくつにすべきなのかしら？

B： 後工程の必要数、化学処理プロセスのロットサイズとリードタイムから発注点を決めるんだ。

A： The final assembly process withdraws one container at a time from the supermarket. One container contains 50 frames. Ten chips are on one frame. After assembly and inspection, they will be contained into one tape-reel every 500 chips.

B： How many types do you have at the chip market?

A： Five types of chips. But when we make 500 chips at a time in the upstream chemical process, we cannot make enough chips in the quantity needed by the downstream, because changeover-time is too long. How should we trigger the production of chips?

B： It is not practical just yet to make 500 chips at a time. You set the Lot-Making Board at the beginning process and make 4,000 chips at a time.

A： We will attach one production kanban on every container at the supermarket, and circulate production kanban between the supermarket and the Lot-Making Board. What will be the trigger point on the Board?

B： You can get it from the quantity needed by the downstream, the lot size and the lead time of the chemical process.

平準化
What is Heijunka?

 ## 平準化はトヨタ生産方式の大前提
──TPS relies on heijunka as a foundation.

平準化とは、「売れ」に合わせて、生産量と機種をともに均す（ならす）こと。そのまま英語にすると "level（平らにする）"ですが、「量と種類をともに」を理解してもらうために、テクニカル・タームとして、あえて日本語の "heijunka" を使うことをお勧めします。平準化は、トヨタ生産方式の大前提。ほかの手法を解説する時と同様に、平準化も、トヨタ生産方式のゴールや2本柱について復習してから説明するとよいでしょう。

平準化とは

平準化とは、生産する量と機種を、ある一定の期間で均すということを意味します。たとえば、午前中にAだけを組み立てて、午後にはBを組み立てる、ということをせず、AとBを小さなバッチで交互につくるのです。

What is Heijunka?

Heijunka means leveling the type and quantity of production over a fixed period of time. For example, instead of assembling all the type A products in the morning and all the type B products in the afternoon, we would alternate small batches of A and B.

なぜ平準化するのか？

平準化すれば、まとめづくりをせずに、「売れ」に合わせてムダなく生産できるようになり、結果として、モノの流れの全体にわたって、最少の在庫、資金、工数、リードタイムを実現できるのです。

Why should we do Heijunka?

Heijunka enables production to efficiently meet customer demands while avoiding batching, and results in minimum inventories, capital costs, manpower, and production lead time through the whole value stream.

◇まとめ生産と平準化生産を比べてみよう

まとめ生産は効率が良い？

組立部門では、ほとんどの人が、できるだけ長く同じ機種の製品をつくり続け、機種切替えを避けることがよいと考えています。しかし、この方が、結局は高くつくのです。

Is batch production truly efficient?

Many assembly departments think it is easier to schedule long runs of one product type and avoid changeovers. However, we end up paying heavily.

まとめ生産と平準化生産を比べてみよう！

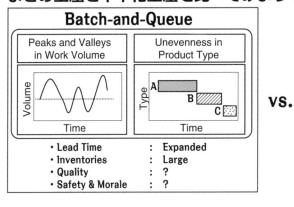

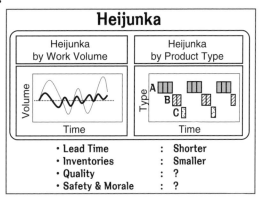

まとめ生産と平準化生産の意味を簡単に説明した後、「どちらがリードタイムが短いと思いますか？」「在庫水準はどうですか？」「品質はどちらが良くなると思いますか？」「働く人にとっては？」などと問いかけ、自ら考えてもらうことで、さらに理解が深まるはずです。

リードタイムは？

バッチ生産では、リードタイムは長くなり、今つくっているバッチの機種とは違う機種が欲しいお客様への対応は難しくなります。そして、お客様が求める機種を、常に持っていたいと思うなら、完成品在庫を増やさなければなりません。

How about Lead time?

Batch production expands lead times. So it becomes difficult to serve customers who want something different than the batch we are making now. Therefore, we have to invest in our finished goods supermarket in hope that we will have what the customer wants on hand.

材料や部品は？

まとめてつくるということは、材料も部品もまとめて使うということであり、仕掛品の在庫をふくらませることになります。

How about Materials and Parts?

Batch production also means that we consume raw materials and parts in batches, which swells WIP inventories.

品質は？

まとめ生産は不良を覆い隠してしまいます。不良をつくっても、そのバッチをつくっている間（には発見できず）、不良をつくり続けてしまいます。このため、品質が良くならないのです。

How about Quality?

Batch production hides defects. Quality suffers because a single defect becomes replicated throughout the batch.

働く人にとっては？

まとめ生産では、作業者は、あるラインはとても忙しいのに、ほかのラインは遊んでいる、というような目に遭います。このやり方はムダが多く、また、仕事にムラがあるとムリが生じ、ムリは安全やモラールも蝕んでしまうのです。

How about impact on workers?

Workers experience unevenness——that is, some lines are very busy, others idle——which also degrades efficiency. The unevenness in the work creates strain, which corrodes safety and morale.

在庫を持つ機種と受注生産する機種を決める──ABC Production Analysis──

まとめ生産から平準化生産へ転換するための第1歩は、在庫を持つ機種と受注生産する機種を決めることです。ご存知の通り、ABC分析を基にして決定します。以下に例を挙げます。

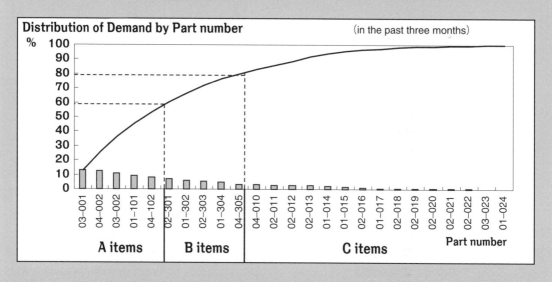

The bars in the diagram show the fraction of total demand accounted by each part number. The curved line running from left to right stacks the orders to show the fraction demand accounted for by any given number of products. In the above example, the first five part numbers account for 60 % of total demand and the first 10 account for 80 %.

A items are high runners, B items are medium runners, and C items are low runners.

Options for Finished Goods vs. Make-to-Order　何を在庫し、何を受注生産するか？

		Options　選択肢	Pros　よい点	Cons　課題
①		Hold finished-goods inventory of all of products (As, Bs, and Cs) and make all to stock – **replenishment pull system.** **後補充生産**(完成品在庫への後補充)	Ready to ship all items on short notice すべての機種で短納期対応が可能になる	Requires space and inventory of every item 全機種について在庫を持つ必要があり、スペースが必要
②		Hold no finished-goods inventory and make all products to order – **sequential pull system.** **順序生産**(在庫を持たず受注生産)	Less inventory and associated waste 在庫と在庫に関連するムダを削減できる	Requires high process stability and short lead time to produce 工程の安定化と、生産リードタイム短縮が求められる
③	ⓐ	Hold only Cs in inventory and make A and B products to order daily – **mixed pull system.** Cは後補充、A，Bを順序生産	Less inventory 在庫を少なくすることができる	Requires mixed production control and daily stability 後補充＋順序生産のきちんとした管理と、日次の安定化が必要
	ⓑ	Hold A and B productsin finished-goods inventory. Make Cs to order from semi-finished components – **mixed pull system.** A，Bは後補充、Cを順序生産	Moderate inventory 在庫を抑えることができる(①案よりは少ないが、②案よりは多い)	Requires mixed production control and visibility on C items 後補充＋順序生産のきちんとした管理と、Cの見える化が必要

How much of each item should we hold in finished goods?
完成品在庫の量を決める

Finished-Goods Calculation Formula			
	Average daily demand × Lead time to replenish（days）	Cycle stock	
+	Demand variation as % of Cycle stock	Buffer stock	
+	Safety factor as % of（Cycle stock＋Buffer stock）	Safety stock	
=		Finished-goods inventory	

Finished goods
Supermarket

Tip:Try holding your safety separately from cycle and buffer stock…use it only in emergencies!

Let's talk   平準化に向けて

A： ABC分析をして、AとBは後補充、Cは受注生産の「組合せ型プル」にすると決めました。また、Cは小さな専用セルでつくることにしました。次はどうすればよいですか？

A： After doing an ABC production analysis, we have decided to employ mixed pull and hold finished goods for A and B items. We have also decided on having a dedicated small cell for C items. What should we do next?

B： AとBの完成品在庫の量を決めるんだ。品番ごとに算出する。こんなふうにね（上図）。

B： You have to decide the initial finished goods inventory levels for A and B. Calculate it for each item in this way（see above formula）.

A： じゃ、計算してみますね。……わぁ！　今まで、在庫をあまりにも多く持ち過ぎていたっていうことが、改めてわかったわ。

A： Okay, I'll calculate them. … Oh! I see that we had been keeping too much inventory.

B： わかってくれたかな？　在庫を抑えながら後補充をきちんとするためには、異常がすぐわかるようにすることがとても大切なんだよ。

B： Did you get it? So, it is crucial to make "normal or abnormal" clear, in order to maintain your inventory levels and replenishment.

A： 次は生産の指示をどうするか、ですよね？

A： Now, we have to discuss how to control production, don't we?

B： その通り。まず、「ペースメーカー」の考え方をしっかり理解する必要があるんだよ。

B： You are right. You need to get a fix on the concept of the "Pacemaker" first.

A： ペースメーカー？　以前に聞いたことがあるわ。……この場合なら、最終工程の組立検査よね？

A： Pacemaker? Oh, I have heard about it from you before. … It must be the final process, assembly and inspection, in this case.

ペースメーカー
What is a Pacemaker?

生産指示を1カ所だけに出す──ペースメーカー

ペースメーカーとは

1つの製品群のバリュー・ストリーム上で、流れの全体に拍動を与えるただ1つの場所のこと。ペースメーカー工程だけが、生産管理部門から生産指示を受け取るのです。

ペースメーカー選定の考え方

ペースメーカー工程は、通常、バリュー・ストリームの最下流の顧客に近い場所です。多くの場合、最終組立工程がこれに該当します。もっと上流の工程をペースメーカーとすることも可能ですが、これは当該上流工程からバリュー・ストリームの最下流まで、先入れ先出しが保たれることを前提とするものです。

注意！　ネック工程とは違う

ペースメーカー工程を、ボトルネック工程と混同してはなりません。

What is a pacemaker?

It means a single point along a value stream that sets the pace for the entire stream. Only the pacemaker process receives the schedule from the production control operation.

Which process should we designate?

The pacemaker process usually is near the customer end of the value stream, often the final assembly area. Any upstream process can be a pacemaker, provided that products flow from this upstream process to the end of the value stream in a FIFO (First in, First out) sequence.

Do not confuse it with a bottleneck process.

The pacemaker process should not be confused with a bottleneck process.

◇なぜペースメーカー工程を決めるのか？

伝統的な押し込み生産 ·························

MRPのような伝統的なスケジューリングでは、それぞれの工程に対して、いっせいに生産指示を出します。この方法は、どれが正しい計画なのかわからないという混乱を生むとともに、結果としてつくり過ぎの原因にもなるものです。

Traditional Push

In a traditional scheduling, such as MRP, multiple schedules are sent to each process. This method causes confusion over the "right" schedule and results in overproduction.

伝統的なスケジューリングと、ペースメーカーへの生産指示（後補充の例）

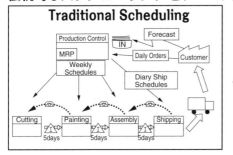

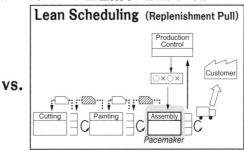

vs.

1カ所だけに生産指示を出す …………………

ペースメーカー工程を1カ所に決めれば、バリュー・ストリーム上の誰もが1つの同じ拍動——つまりペースメーカーのタクトタイムに合わせて、仕事をすることができるようになります。

Only the pacemaker receives the schedule.

Selecting a single point as the pacemaker enables everyone along the value stream to keep working to the same beat, the takt time at the pacemaker.

◇ペースメーカー工程におけるバッチサイズ

先に説明した「平準化」は、ペースメーカー工程に対する生産指示においてこそ、最初になされるべきものなのです。ペースメーカー工程が大バッチのままであったなら、バリュー・ストリーム全体の在庫は、伝統的なまとめと押し込みの時代と大差ないレベルにとどまってしまうでしょう。

お客様が求める荷姿（収容数）に着目する ………

収容数とは、運搬と出荷に際し、1コンテナに入れるようお客様が求めている数のことです。ペースメーカーにおけるバッチサイズは、この収容数と同じか、その倍数にすることが目標です。

How much is the customer Pack-Out Quantity?

Pack-Out Quantity means the number of products that a customer requires packed in a container for transportation and shipping. It is the goal to produce products in the pacemaker process in the same batch size as the Pack-Out-Quantity or any multiple of it.

ペースメーカー工程のバッチサイズを決める ………

理想的なのは、バッチサイズをお客様の収容数の単位と同じにすることです。しかし、段取り時間の長さや、機種間の作業量の差異のために、多くの企業にとって、これは困難です。ペースメーカーのバッチサイズは、下記を慎重に考慮して決めるべきです。

- 作業量の機種間のバラツキ
- 段取り時間
- ピッチ・インターバル

What should be the pacemaker batch size?

An ideal method is to produce products in the same size as the Pack-Out Quantity. But this is very difficult for many processes because of their long changeover times and work content differences between products. It should be determined after carefully evaluating below :

- Work content differences between products
- Changeover times
- Pitch Interval

いよいよ平準化！でもその前に——The pacemaker should produce in a continuous flow.

いよいよペースメーカー工程での平準化に挑戦するところまで来ました！　しかし、ちょっと待って下さい。ペースメーカー工程は、流れ化されていなければなりません。ペースメーカー工程をもう一度よく見て、次の2点を確認しましょう。

①流れ化されているか？

　ペースメーカー工程は、流れ化されている必要があります。流れ化とは、強制駆動ラインか、または流れ化セル（またはライン）を意味します。これができていないなら、平準化は困難です。1つ戻ってもっと流れ改善に取り組むべきです。

② Has continuous flow been established?

The operations in the pacemaker process should be arranged in a continuous flow. This may mean a moving conveyor line, or a continuous flow cell (or line). If it has been designed poorly, it will be difficult for you to implement a level pull system. In this case, you should take a backward step and make another try at flow kaizen.

②可動率は75％以上か？

　ペースメーカー工程での可動率は、少なくとも75％以上であることが求められます。これができていないなら、まず真因を追及し、問題を解決しなければなりません。

② Is the operational availability at least 75%?

The operational availability of the pacemaker process should be 75% or greater, at least. If not, you should first identify the root causes of the poor availability and solve the problems.

ペースメーカー工程には、必ずアンドンを！—Try Andon to spot abnormalities!—

ペースメーカー工程では、バッチサイズを小さくし、段取り替えを頻繁に行いながら製造することが求められます。この結果、人々は、押し込み生産の時代には気にならなかった小さなトラブル（チョコ停、不良発生、部品異常、作業の遅れ等々）に直面することになります。つまり、押し込み生産の時代に比べて、もっと素早く問題に対処することが必要になるのです。もうわかりましたね？　ペースメーカー工程にはアンドンを必ず付けましょう！

アンドンは、現場の状態がステーションごとにひと目でわかるように表示し、また何か異常があればすぐに知らせることができる、目で見る管理の道具です。
ひもスイッチとアンドンを組み合わせることで、素早く問題を発見し、対処することができるようになります。

Andon is a visual management tool to highlight the status of operations in each station at a single glance, and to tell you immediately whenever something abnormal occurs.
Employing an andon with a signal cord, you will be able to identify the problems immediately and to take measures against them quickly.

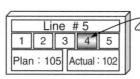

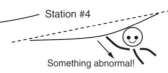

Station #4

ひもスイッチ
Signal Cord

Something abnormal!

Leveling quantity and product-mix at the pacemaker
ペースメーカー工程で、量と機種を平準化する

Batch Size for each category			Demand per day：1,220 pieces 7.5hrs./day, 3shifts/day, Takt Time：66 sec.			
Product Category	Number of items	Demand	QTY. per day	Pitch Interval	Batch Size	EPE
A item	8	60%	720	36	80	1 day
B item	8	20%	240	12	60	2 days
C item	13	20%	260	13	40	2 days
Total	29	100%	1,220	61		

Production Control

Heijunka Box
○ × ○ ×

Customer

Pacemaker

Assembly
Continuous Flow

Let's talk ペースメーカーで平準化した生産指示を出す

A： 最終組立ラインの段取り改善の結果、段取り替えが 2 分以内でできるようになりました。

B： それはすごいよ！　サイクルタイムのバラツキはどのくらいあるの？

A： タクトタイムは66秒、サイクルタイムは最短で56秒、最長で66秒です。ですから、このラインで、この製品群の全機種を平準化して流せますよね。

B： それで、この差立板をつくったんだね？　66秒×20個/トレーだから、ピッチは1,320秒、22分か……。これも平準化を始めるのにはちょうどいいね。

A： これが機種ごとのバッチサイズです。毎日注文がある機種は毎日つくります。これが8機種あります。そのほかの機種は2日に1回つくります。

B： 水すましのルートと作業は分析した？

A： はい、15分です。

A： We have improved changeover time in final assembly line and can now change settings for each item within two minutes.

B： Good work! Now, how much difference is there in cycle time between items?

A： Takt time is 66 seconds. The shortest cycle time is 56 seconds and the longest one takes 66 seconds. So, we are going to produce all items for this family on this line, leveling both quantity and product-mix.

B： Then, you made this heijunka box, didn't you? Multiplying the takt time of 66 seconds by the pack quantity of 20 pieces will show the pitch to be 1,320 seconds, or 22 minutes……. So this is a great place to start heijunka.

A： These are the batch sizes for each item. We will produce every day items are ordered by the customer. They are eight of those items. Others will be produced every two days.

B： Have you evaluated the mizusumashi route and work contents through your trials?

A： Yes. The route is 15 minutes.

Chapter

3

自働化と設備改善
Jidoka and Machines

自働化
What is Jidoka ?

👷 自働化とは？

自働化とは、よく知られている通り、不良が発生したら（あるいは発生しそうになったら）ただちに停止すること。ジャスト・イン・タイムとともに、トヨタ生産方式の２本柱を構成する重要な概念です。本書でも今までに説明してきましたが、自働化の説明では、自動停止やひもスイッチなどのテクニカルな説明に先立ち、豊田佐吉翁の自動織機と歴史的経緯、なぜ自働化が大切なのか、といった基本事項を丁寧に説明することが必要でしょう。なお、昨今は、英語圏でも日本語の"jidoka"をそのまま使うケースが増えています。英語のみで表現する時は、"intelligent automation"や"automation with human touch"、あるいは"autonomous"からの造語"autonomation"を用いる場合が多いようです。

自働化とは？
自働化とは、異常発生を検知して即座に停止し、対策をとる機能を、設備と作業者に与えることを意味します。

なぜ自働化が求められるのか？
設備やプロセスが自働化されていなければ、不良を防ぐために、作業者は設備を見張っていなければなりません。自働化によって、各プロセスで品質をつくり込むことができ、人と設備の動きを分けて、よりムダのない働きとすることができるのです。

「人と機械の仕事を分ける」ことが、なぜ大切なのか？
機械の見張り番から作業者を解放すれば、機械が加工している間に、作業者に付加価値を生む別の仕事をしてもらうことができます。たとえば、機械の多台持ちや多工程持ちです。

What is Jidoka ?
Jidoka means providing machines and operators the ability to detect when an abnormal situation has occurred and immediately stop work to institute countermeasures.

Why should we adopt Jidoka ?
Where machines and processes do not equip themselves with jidoka, operators are needed to keep watch on machines to prevent defects. Jidoka enables operations to build in quality at each process and to separate operators from machines for more efficient work.

What can we achieve through separating human work from machine work ?
Freeing operators from simply monitoring machines through jidoka enables operators to do other value-creating work during machine cycle, for example, multi-machine handling and multi-process handling.

Jidoka originated from the auto loom invented by Mr.Sakichi Toyoda in the early 20th Century.

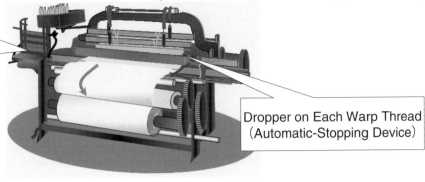

Automatic Shuttle Changer
（Pushing-Slider）

Dropper on Each Warp Thread
（Automatic-Stopping Device）

◇自働化とジャスト・イン・タイムのルーツ
──Two Great Creators in modern Japan.

自働化とジャスト・イン・タイムのルーツは、ともに戦前（第2次世界大戦前）にあります。トヨタグループの社祖である豊田佐吉翁（1867～1930）は、20世紀初頭に自動織機を発明し、後に自働化と呼ばれることになる概念を具現化しました。佐吉翁の子息であり、トヨタ自動車の創業者・豊田喜一郎氏（1894～1952）は、1930年代にジャスト・イン・タイムの概念を提唱しました。

Jidoka and just-in-time both have their roots in the prewar (pre-WWII) period. In the early 20th Century, Mr. Sakichi Toyoda (1867-1930), founder of the Toyota Group, realized the concept of jidoka, as important aspects of his invention of an automatic loom. Mr. Kiichiro Toyoda (1894-1952), son of Sakichi and founder of Toyota automobile business, developed the concept of just-in-time in the 1930's.

◇佐吉翁の自動織機──The auto loom invented by Mr.Sakichi Toyoda.

佐吉翁は、経（たて）糸が切れたら自動停止する自動織機を発明しました。この自動織機は、横糸がなくなる直前にシャトル（杼・ひ）を自動排出し、新たなシャトルを自動供給する機構も備えていました。この間も織機はフルスピードで動き続け、止まることはありませんでした。（無停止）

Sakichi Toyoda invented an automatic loom that would stop automatically for problems. He equipped his loom with the ability to stop whenever a warp thread broke and to eject almost-empty shuttles quickly and then insert a new one at the last second before the weft thread in each shuttle was completely consumed, all while the machine was operating at full speed. It enabled great improvement in quality and freed operators to do more value-creating work than simply monitoring auto looms.

これによって、品質において劇的な改善が得られるとともに、織機に張り付くことから作業者を解放し、付加価値を生む別の仕事をしてもらうこともできるようになったのです。
その後、異常が発生したら自動停止し、異常を知らせるように設備を設計するという考え方は、トヨタのあらゆる設備、あらゆるライン、あらゆる仕事のやり方において、不可欠なものとなりました。

Eventually the concept of designing machines to stop automatically and call immediate attention to problems became a critical feature of every machine, every production line, and every Toyota operation.

自働化のステップ——Levels of Jidoka

佐吉翁の事跡に学び、まずは加工のプロセスをよく観察することから、自働化へのステップは始まります。この時、人の動きと機械の動きを分けて見ることが大切です。

	Load	Start	Machine Cycle	Stop Normal	Stop Abnormal	Unload
1	☺	☺	☺	☺	☺	☺
2	☺	☺	Auto	☺	☺	☺
3	☺	☺	Auto	Auto	☺	☺
4	☺	☺	Auto	Auto	Auto	☺
5	☺	☺	Auto	Auto	Auto	Auto
6	☺	Auto	Auto	Auto	Auto	Auto
7	Auto	Auto	Auto	Auto	Auto	Auto

面対照配置の自動織機が多台持ちを加速した

——Mirror-Symmetric setting of Toyoda Auto Looms boosted Multi-Machine Handling.

豊田式自動織機は面対照の配置が可能でした。これにより、シャトル供給作業と織機の再スタート動作の場所が近接化され、作業者の動作のムダを省き、より多くの多台持ちができるようになったのです。

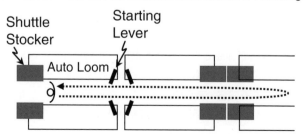

Shuttle Stocker
Starting Lever
Auto Loom

What a lavish expenditure of human ability!

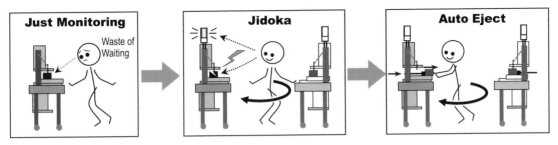

| Just Monitoring | Jidoka | Auto Eject |

Let's talk　　　もったいないっ !!

A : 組立セルでは、タクトタイムより少しだけ短いサイクルで、安定してつくれるようになったんですよ、ほら。

B : あーっ！　もったいないっ！

A : モ…モッタイナイ？　それは何？

B : 「もったいない」は、「わぁ、これって、ものすごくムダだよね！」っていうような意味なんだよ。ほら、溶接の作業者は、機械が動いている間、付加価値を付ける動作を何もしてないよね？

A : その通りなんだけど、仕方がないわ。不良が発生するかもしれないし。それに、部品を取り付けて、取り外す人は必要ですもの。

B : それは人の能力のムダ遣い。「もったいない」の1つだよ。自働化の話を覚えているかな？

A : あ、ジドウカ、つまり異常があったら自動停止ですね！　教わったことがあります。でも、取付けと取外しがあるから、彼女の手待ちの時間はそんなに長くはないわ。

B : そこで、「ハネ出し」の出番なんだ。

A : Here, our assembly cell has been improved to operate stably with the cycle time a little shorter than the takt time.

B : Whoa! Mottai-Nai!!

A : Mo…. Mottah-i-Na-i?　What do you mean?

B : "Mottai-nai" means "How wasteful!" You see that the operator at the welding process really does nothing value-creating during machine cycle, don't you?

A : Yes, you are right. But there is no alternative, because the machine might make defects. And someone needs to set parts and pick them up.

B : It is a great lavish expenditure of human ability. This is one Mottai-nai—very wasteful—practice. Do you remember jidoka?

A : Oh, jidoka, or automatic-machine-stop to prevent abnormalities！ We have learned about it. But the loading-and-unloading work does not give her long waiting time.

B : Then, we come to an auto-eject device.

稼働率と可動率
Operating Rate vs. Operational Availability

稼働率と可動率とは？

稼働率は皆さんご存知の通り。可動率とは、TPSの進化と深化の過程で考え出された考え方の1つで、設備やシステムが動いてほしいときに、どのくらい正しく動いているかを示す指標です。稼働率と区別するため、「べきどうりつ」とも読みます。近年は、TPMに取り組む海外生産拠点も増えていますが、そのような工場では、今までの彼らの改善の蓄積を活かす説明が求められるでしょう。

稼働率とは？
稼働率とは、ある期間（シフト、日など）に、設備が何かをつくるために使われている時間が、どのくらいあるかを示すものです。

可動率とは？
可動率とは、設備が必要なときに正しく動く割合です。

高稼働率のワナ
高い設備稼働率を維持するのは一見よいことのように感じられますが、後工程が必要としているか否かに関係なく設備を動かすのなら、それはつくり過ぎのムダを生むことになります。稼働率は、お客様である後工程が求める量に応じて、高くも低くもなるものです。

可動率は100％が理想
高い稼働率は常によいとは言えませんが、可動率は100％が理想です。

Operating Rate
The operating rate means the amount of time in a time frame (shift, day, etc.) that a machine is used to make something.

Operational Availability
The operational availability is the fraction of time that a machine functions properly when needed.

The trap of chasing high operating rate
Keeping a high operating rate sounds effective on the surface, but it often causes the waste of overproduction when we run machines without relation to any need of the processes downstream. The operating rate may be high or low according to the need of its customers, or the processes downstream.

The ideal operational availability is 100%.
A high operating rate is not necessarily desirable, but the ideal operational availability rate should be 100%.

Operating Rate vs. Operational Availability〜稼働率と可動率

Operating Rate　稼働率

$$\frac{\text{Actual run-time}}{\text{Available production time}}$$

Actual run-time
（実際に動いていた時間）

Available production time
（想定する稼働時間）

VS.

Operational Availability　可動率

Cycle time * × **Required qty.**
（必要数に対して決められた所要時間）

Actual time to produce
（実際にかかった時間）

*Cycle time does not include any failures, adjustments, minor stoppages, or defects in this calculation.

◇設備総合効率── Overall Equipment Effectiveness

設備総合効率とは？

設備総合効率は、TPMの重要な指標の1つで、設備がどのくらいムダなく使われているかを示すものです。設備総合効率は、3つの要素の掛け算で計算されます。

　時間稼働率×性能稼働率×良品率

Overall Equipment Effectiveness (OEE)

OEE is one of the essential TPM (Total Productive Maintenance) metrics. It measures how effectively equipment is being used. OEE is calculated through the multiplication of three elements:

　Availability Rate × Performance rate × Quality Rate.

※上記（右段）英訳語の"Availability Rate"（時間稼働率のTPM英訳語）は、"可動率＝Operational Availability"とイコールではないことに留意して下さい（可動率は、〔時間稼働率×性能稼働率〕の意味で使われたり、OEEとほぼ同じ意味で使われることも多い概念です）。

設備の6大ロス

① 故障
② 段取り
③ チョコ停
④ 速度ロス
⑤ 不良
⑥ 手直し

※上記以外にもさまざまなロスを採用している企業・組織があります。

The Six Major Losses in Machinery

① Breakdown
② Changeovers and Adjustments
③ Minor Stoppages
④ Speed Losses
⑤ Scrap
⑥ Rework

※ Some companies and associations employ additional metrics.

作業者も保全の一翼を担う

保全担当者による従来の予防保全とは異なり、TPMでは、作業者を巻き込み、日常の保全や改善活動、簡単な修理も作業者が行うことを目指します。たとえば、潤滑油のチェックと補充、清掃、増締め、設備の点検などです。

TPM involves production workers in maintenance activities.

Unlike traditional PM, which relies on skilled maintenance personnel, TPM involves operators in routine maintenance, kaizen activities and simple repairs, such as lubricating, cleaning, tightening, and inspecting machines.

なぜを5回繰り返せ！——The Five Whys

「5回のなぜ」とは、問題に出会ったら、常に目に見える現象を超えて、真因に到達するまで「なぜ？」を繰り返すべし、という意味です。

その著作「トヨタ生産方式」(1978、ダイヤモンド社)に書かれた大野耐一氏の「5回のなぜ」を復習しましょう。

1. なぜ機械は止まったか？
   オーバーロードがかかって、ヒューズが切れたからだ。

2. なぜオーバーロードがかかったのか？
   軸受部の潤滑が十分でないからだ。

3. なぜ十分に潤滑しないのか？
   潤滑ポンプが十分にくみ上げていないからだ。

4. なぜ十分くみ上げないのか？
   ポンプの軸が磨耗してガタガタになっているからだ。

5. なぜ磨耗したのか？
   ストレーナー(濾過機)が付いていないので、切粉が入ったからだ。

The phrase "Five Whys" means the practice of asking why repeatedly whenever a problem is encountered in order to get beyond the obvious symptoms to identify the root cause. Let's review the "Five Whys" in "Toyota Production System" written by Mr. Taiichi Ohno (1988, NY. Productivity Press).

1. Why did the machine stop?
   There was an overload and the fuse blew.

2. Why was there an overload?
   The bearing was not sufficiently lubricated.

3. Why was it not lubricated?
   The lubrication pump was not pumping sufficiently.

4. Why was it not pumping sufficiently?
   The shaft of the pump was worn and rattling.

5. Why was the shaft worn out?
   There was no strainer attached and metal scraps got in.

TPSとTPM——TPM originated at Denso, the Toyota Group company.

1971年、日本電装*がJIPE**主催のPM賞を受賞します。この時、同社の設備保全に対する優れた全社的な取組みがJIPEの審査員によって注目されました。これがTPMのルーツとされています。それ以前には、PM活動の多くは保全部門のものと考えられていたのです。

In 1971, Nippondenso* was awarded the distinguished plant prize for PM, by JIPE**. The JIPE auditors were impressed with Nippondenso's company-wide PM activities. The origin of "T" PM has been credited to Nippondenso since that time. Until then, most PM activities had been assigned to skilled maintenance personnel.

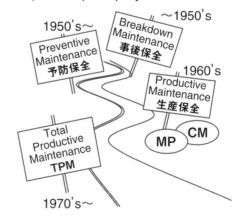

*日本電装 Nippondenso：Former name of Denso (現・㈱デンソー)

**JIPE：Former name of JIPM (現・㈳日本プラントメンテナンス協会)

Reducing minor stoppages reduces lead time, cost and enables an operator to do additional work!

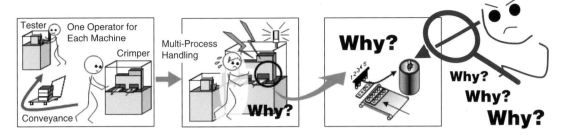

Let's talk　真因に至るまで、現地・現物・現実で追及！

A：金曜日から、カシメ機と検査の多工程持ちを始めましたが、生産量が計画に達しません。

B：この2つは、ラインの最終工程だね？　改善を始める場所としてはまあ正しいよね。…でも、カシメ機のチョコ停がどのくらい起きているか、わかってる？　ほら、またまた止まった！　今すぐ、…そうだなあ、最低でも2時間は、工程をよく観察しなくちゃね！

《…2時間後…》

A：わかりましたよ！　カシメ機では、1度に5個ずつ加工するのですが、3番目のピッキングアームが部品をしょっちゅう取り損なっていたのです。そこで、3番目のヘッドを交換したら、チョコ停がほとんどなくなりました。

B：よかったね。では、3番目のヘッドが部品を取り損なっていたのはどうして？

A：ヘッドのガイド溝が変形していました。理由はわかりませんが…。

B：真因がわかるまで、「なぜ？」を繰り返さなくちゃいけないよ。

A：We have started multi-process handling from the crimping to the testing since Friday, but the output has not reached the target yet.

B：Are these two processes the final ones of this line? It is basically the right place to start. But, do you know how often the crimping machine stops? Now, it has just stopped. And again! You should observe this process from now for at least ...... two hours!

《…Two hours later…》

A：We have turned up a clue! It crimps five work pieces at a time. We found that the third picking-arm often had missed parts. So I replaced its head with a new one. Since then, almost no minor stoppage has occurred.

B：Good! Well, did you get at the reason why the third one had so often missed parts?

A：Its guide-flute had collapsed. We don't know why ...

B：You should repeat more "Whys" until coming to the root cause.

段取り改善
Setup Reduction

😀 なぜ段取り改善が必要なのか？

段取り時間が長ければ、大バッチでつくらざるを得ません。しかし、お客様（後工程）の必要に応えながら在庫を減らしたいと願うなら、答えは1つ、段取り時間の短縮しかないのです。一般に、下流の組立ラインの段取り改善は比較的短期間のうちに実現可能であり、またぜひそうすべきものですが、上流工程のバッチプロセスでは、技術部門はもちろんのこと、設備メーカーも巻き込んだ粘り強い活動が求められます。期間も長期にわたるでしょう。だからこそ、単に「段取り時間を短縮せよ」と指示するのではなく、段取り時間短縮が平準化生産の実現にとって不可欠であり、トータルリードタイム短縮と在庫削減に必ず結び付くという確信を、関係者全員に持ってもらうことが重要なのです。

段取りとは？

段取りとは、単体設備や自動化ラインで、1つの型番の製品または部品の生産から、違う型番の製品または部品の生産に切り替えることを言います。部品やプレス金型、モールド金型、治具などを交換して切り替えるのです。

Changeover

Changeover means the process of switching from the production of one product or part number to another in a machine or a series of linked machines by changing parts, dies, molds, fixtures, etc.

段取り時間とは？

段取り時間とは、最後の1個が完成した後、段取りを行ってから最初の1個目の良品が出てくるまでの時間です。

Changeover Time

Changeover time is measured as the time elapsed between the last piece in the run just completed and the first good piece from the process after the changeover.

ロットを小さく、段取り替えを速やかに

バッチプロセスの段取り時間をシングル（10分以内）まで短縮できるのなら、段取り回数を増やすことによって、後補充のリードタイムを大幅に減らすことができるでしょう。

Producing smaller batches with quick changeovers

You will be able to considerably reduce replenishment lead time in batch process with additional changeovers, if changeover times can be taken down to a single digit, or less than 10 minutes.

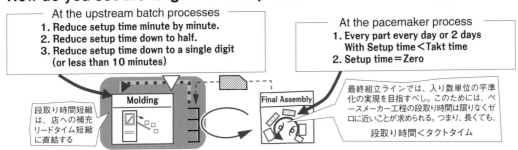

How do you set the targets in Setup Reduction? 〜段取り改善の目標〜

At the upstream batch processes
1. Reduce setup time minute by minute.
2. Reduce setup time down to half.
3. Reduce setup time down to a single digit (or less than 10 minutes)

At the pacemaker process
1. Every part every day or 2 days With Setup time＜Takt time
2. Setup time＝Zero

Molding

Final Assembly

段取り時間短縮は、店への補充リードタイム短縮に直結する

最終組立ラインでは、入り数単位の平準化の実現を目指すべし。このためには、ペースメーカー工程の段取り時間は限りなくゼロに近いことが求められる。つまり、長くても、

段取り時間＜タクトタイム

◇段取り改善の目標をどのように設定するか？

—— How should we set the targets in setup reduction?

「改善はお客様に一番近い最終工程から始める」というセオリー通り、段取り改善もまた最終組立ラインの改善の中に位置付けられ、スタートするはずです。まずは、現在の最終組立ラインの段取り時間を正確に測定することが第1歩。ここでのゴールは、お客様が指定した入り数の単位で平準化できるようになることです。一方、最終組立ラインで改善を始めたばかりの時期でも、上流のバッチプロセスの段取り改善に着手することは大きな意味があります。上流の段取り改善は、下流の工程に比べ、時間もお金もかかる場合が多いからです。

ペースメーカー工程の段取り改善 ....

ペースメーカー工程において、もしも段取り時間がゼロならば、顧客の入り数（収容数）の単位で1機種ずつ切り替えることが可能です。これは理想です。不可能ではありませんが、すぐに実現するのが難しければ、全機種を1日または2日でつくることを最初の目標にしましょう。できるだけ早く、段取り時間をタクトタイム以下まで短縮しなければなりません。

Setup reduction at the pacemaker process

If the setup time is zero at the pacemaker, you can changeover one container by one container in the amount of the Pack-Out quantity. This is the ideal. It is not impossible, but, in such cases where it is hard to immediately realize, you can set the first-stage target to produce every part every day or two days. Then, you should shorten changeover times down to less than the takt time as soon as possible.

上流のバッチプロセスの段取り改善 ....

上流のバッチプロセスでは、最初は、段取り時間を少しずつ短縮することから始めて、次のステップとして半分まで短縮しましょう。さらに、シングル段取り（10分以内）が可能になれば、補充リードタイムを大幅に短縮し、在庫をもっと削減することもできるのです。

Setup reduction at the upstream batch processes

In the beginning at upstream processes, you had better start with reducing current setup times minute by minute. And then, challenge reducing setup times down to half. Eventually, if you can change over within ten minutes, you will significantly shorten your replenishment lead time and reduce your inventories.

段取り改善のステップ ——The Basic Steps in Setup Reduction

この分野では、特に新郷重夫氏（1909～1990）の研究と実践が日本国内のみならず、北米でもよく知られています。新郷氏は、トヨタの人々とともに現場で研究し、「段取り改善のステップ」として、その考え方と技法を整理しました（参考：「シングル段取への原点的志向」（JMA）1983, "A Revolution in Manufacturing : The SMED System"（Productivity Press）, 1985, SMED : "Single Minute Exchange of Die"）。

1．現状の段取り時間を測定する。	1. Measure the setup time in the current state.
2．段取り作業を内段取りと外段取りにハッキリ分化し、それぞれの時間を算出する。	2. Identify the internal and external setup elements, calculating the individual times.
3．内段取り要素を可能な限り外段取りに転化する*。	3. Convert as many of the internal elements to external elements as possible.
4．外段取り化できずに残った内段取り要素の時間を短縮する。	4. Reduce the time for the remaining internal elements.
5．外段取りの時間を短縮する。	5. Reduce the time for the external elements.
6．段取り替えの新手順を、標準作業化する。	6. Standardize the new procedure.

- 内段取り：設備を停止して行う段取り作業

- 外段取り：設備を止めなくても行える段取り作業

*新郷氏の提唱のうち、最も特徴的な部分

- Internal Setup Work

  Internal setup work can be done only when a machine is stopped.

- External Setup Work

  External setup work can be done while a machine is running.

Changeover と Setup　何が違う？

段取り替えは **Changeover** または **Setup**。用語定義へのこだわり過ぎは時間のムダというものですが、段取り改善については、下記を覚えておくと役立つかもしれません。

- もともと、**Changeover** は品目を切り替えるという意味。**Setup** は具体的な段取り替えの作業そのものを表す。
- よって、「頻繁な段取り替え」は "**frequent changeovers**"、「素早い段取り替え」は "**quick changeover**"。
- 段取り作業の改善なら "**setup reduction**" がピッタリくる一方で、たとえば「在庫を減らすには段取り時間短縮が必須」といった「概念としての品目切り替え」を表すなら、"**reducing changeover time（s）**" も自然な表現となる。
- ここで、"**reducing changeover（s）**" と time を省略してしまうと、段取り「時間」短縮ではなく「回数」の削減という反対の意味に受け取られてしまう可能性があり、（特に会話では）要注意。

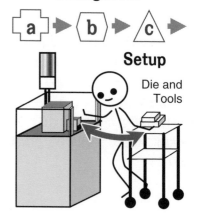

Changeover

a ► b ► c ►

Setup

Die and Tools

Identifying Internal and External Setup Work is the first clue to reducing changeover time.

Printer Setup (Current)
1. Stop printer
2. Walk to screen rack
3. Get next screen & tools
4. Walk back to the printer
5. Drain remaining graphite
6. Get current-item screen off
7. Set next screen
8. Adjust screen
9. Clean previous screen up
10. Bring back screen & tools to rack

Let's talk　まずは外段取り化！

A： スクリーン印刷工程には、まだ問題が残っています。品目切り替えに約40分かかっているのです。

B： そのおかげで、印刷機の後ろにこんなに在庫を持たなくてはならないんだね。それで、タクトタイムと印刷時間は？

A： タクトタイムは1秒/個、シート1枚50個を一度に印刷します。シート1枚当たりの印刷時間は40秒です。

B： 必要な能力がシフト当たり540シートだよね。540シート印刷するのには360分かかるから、シフト当たり、切り替えに使える時間が90分はある、と。で、これを切り替え時間の40分で割ると…う〜ん、シフト当たり2回しか切り替えられないってことか。

A： だから段取り時間短縮が必要なんですよね。まず何をしたらよいでしょう？

B： まずは、外段取りを分けることだね。ほら、作業者が機械を止めてから、スクリーンと工具を取りに行ったでしょう？

A： There are problems remaining at the screen-printing process. It takes about 40 minutes to change printing items over.

B： So it makes you keep all this inventory next to the screen printer. OK, let me know the takt time and the printing time.

A： The takt time is one second per piece and 50 pieces on each sheet are printed at a time. The printing cycle time is 40 seconds per sheet.

B： 540 sheets are required per shift. It takes 360 minutes to produce 540 sheets. Then you have 90 minutes to change the screen over every shift. Dividing 90 minutes by changeover-time 40 minutes, um.., you can currently change the printer over only twice every shift.

A： So we really need to reduce changeover time. What should we do first?

B： First of all, you should separate the external setup elements from the setup work. You can see that the operator is going to get the next item's screen and tools after stopping the printer.

人と機械の仕事を分ける
Separating Human Work and Machine Work

👦 人の能力を最大限に引き出すには？

人は、今見えている状態よりも、ずっと大きな能力を発揮する可能性を秘めています。しかし、現実には、作業者の多くに手待ちがある一方で、ほとんどの工程につくり過ぎがあります。人の能力のムダ遣いを減らし、人の能力を最大限に引き出すため、機械から人を離す工夫が必要です。

人と機械の仕事を分けることが第1歩

人と機械の仕事を分けることは、1人ひとりの作業者の能力を最大限に発揮してもらうための第1歩です。

工程をじっと見る

まず、作業者の手元がよく見える位置に立って、じっと観察しましょう。加工の順序に沿って、人の仕事、機械の仕事を分けて、それぞれの時間を測定します。

自動化で手待ちをなくす

作業者の手待ちの時間や、単に機械を監視しているだけの時間に着目します。自動化すれば、異常の検知やミスの防止のために人が機械を監視する必要はなくなることに気づくでしょう。

すべての機械にハネ出しを

それが可能と思えるところならどこにでも、ハネ出しを付けましょう。ハネ出しは、人を機械から離すのに大きな力となるでしょう。

Maximize Human Ability

Separating human work and machine work is the first step to maximize the abilities of the individual operators.

Close Observation of Process

First of all, stand where you can see both operator's hands well and study the process carefully. Separate the operator's work elements and machine cycle according to the process sequence, and then time each of them.

Jidoka to Reduce Waiting Time

Look at waiting and simply-monitoring times. You can understand that operators will have no need to simply monitor machines equipped with jidoka to detect abnormalities and avoid making mistakes.

Auto Eject for All Machines

You should apply auto eject everywhere possible. It will greatly help to separate operators from machines.

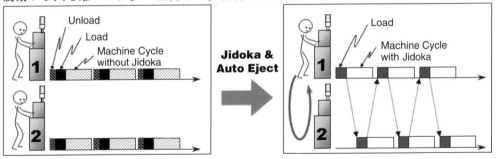

Freeing operators from machines makes Multi-Process/Machine-Handling possible.
機械から人を離せば、多工程持ちや多台持ちが可能になる！

◇設備の能力最大化 vs. 人の能力最大化
—— Maximizing the Utilization of Machines vs. Maximizing the Abilities of Operators

「高い設備稼働率を維持すれば原価が下がる」という伝統的な考え方は、素材産業や上流のバッチプロセス型の現場では、今なお適切と言えるかもしれません。しかし、最終顧客に近づけば近づくほど、設備稼働率の最大化がつくり過ぎに直結する危険は増大します。下流のプロセスでは、設備稼働率最大化よりも、人の能力を最大限に引き出すことが求められます。国内・海外を問わず、人離しのテクニック以前の問題として、この考え方をよく理解してもらうことが重要です。

人、設備、モノのトレードオフ
工程の設計において、人、設備、モノは、トレードオフの関係にあります。3つのうち1つの効率を最大化しようとすると、残り2つの効率は下がってしまいます。

Tradeoffs in People, Machines and Materials
There are tradeoffs between people, machines and materials in designing a process. If you try to maximize one of these three elements, the utilization of the other two is to decline.

設備稼働率を最大化すると？
設備稼働率を最大化する、つまりトップスピードで安定して設備を動かそうとするなら、余分な作業者と余分な仕掛りが必要です。

Maximize Machine Utilization?
Maximizing the utilization of machines or trying to run them constantly at their maximum speed requires extra operators and extra inventory.

モノの効率を最大化（＝在庫をゼロに）すると？
モノの効率を最大化するとは在庫ゼロという意味です。在庫をゼロにしようとするなら、需要変動に対応するために余分な作業者と余分な設備が必要です。

Maximize Material Utilization?
Maximizing the utilization of materials means zero-inventory. If you try to realize this, you will need extra operators and extra machines to meet demand fluctuations.

人の効率を最大化するなら？
おもしろいことに、人の能力を最大化すると、新たな解を得ることも可能です。設備に比べて、人間はとてもフレキシブルだからです。

Maximize Operator Utilization?
Interestingly, maximizing the utilization of operators can lead you to some new solutions, because humans are much more flexible than machines.

人離しの切り札、ハネ出し！

—— Auto Eject, as leverage to separate people from machines

ハネ出しとは、ワークの自動排出機構を設備に付けること。これは、人を機械から離すために欠かせないテクニックです。ワークを排出するのは取り付ける機構よりも安く実現できることが多く、これもハネ出しの特長です。

Auto eject is a technique to equip a machine with an automatic unloading device. Auto eject is crucial to free operators from simply waiting until the end of machine cycles. It is highly useful in that you can equip various machines with auto eject devices at relatively lower costs than loading devices.

ハネ出しと人の動き Operator's movement before/after Auto Eject

	Procedure (assuming both hands handling)	Operator's Movement	
		Before Auto Eject	with Auto Eject
1	Bring a new work piece to the machine. 新しいワークを設備まで運ぶ	☺	☺
2	Lay it down temporarily near the machine. 持ってきたワークを設備の近くに一時的に置く	☹	—
3	Pick a finished work piece up and lay it down. 完成品を設備から取り出し、一時的に取り置く	☹	—
4	Pick up the new work piece. 新しいワークを取る	☹	—
5	Set the new work piece into machine. 新しいワークを設備にセットする	☺	☺
6	Push the start-button of machine. 設備のスタートボタンを押す	☺	☺
7	Machine Cycle マシンサイクル	—	—
8	Pick up the finished work piece from the temporary place and bring it to the next process. 完成品を一時的な置き場から取り、次工程へ運ぶ	☺	☺

※ 上の表は両手でなければ持てないワークを想定したもの。 2〜4項のムダが特に目立つ。
※ Assuming both-hands work, the double-handling in above procedures #2-4 are easy to spot.

チャクチャクをどう言う？ ——a Chaku-Chaku Line

ハネ出しを説明したら、チャクチャクについても言及したくなるのが人情というもの。しかし、英語での定番表現は存在しないようです。日本語のチャクチャクをそのまま使って、"Chaku-Chaku means 'loading-loading' in Japanese"。本物のラインで、チャクチャク動作をシミュレーションしてみるのも、理解を深めるのに役立つでしょう。

Eject Arm automatically pushes a finished good work piece to eject. Any defects are not to be ejected.

Operator does not have to remove finished work pieces from machine. He/she needs simply to load after loading.

Our goal is maximizing the abilities of people! ハネ出しは手段、目的は？

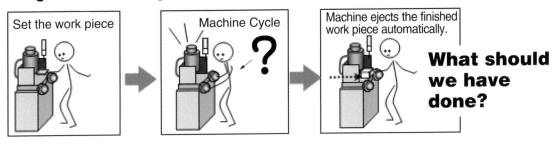

Set the work piece

Machine Cycle ?

Machine ejects the finished work piece automatically.

What should we have done?

Let's talk　目的は、機械から人を離すこと！

A：ハネ出しのコンセプトをフォーミング機に適用しました。

B：なるほどね…。う〜ん、惜しいなあ。ほら、彼女、フォーミングサイクルの間ずっと、両手で起動ボタンを押し続けなくちゃいけないっていう問題が、残ったままだよ。

A：しかし、両手スイッチは安全基準ですから、変えるのはちょっと…。

B：このままでは、ハネ出しを活かすことができないよ。彼女を機械から解放しなくちゃ。安全のためならエリアセンサやシャッターを使って、起動はリミットスイッチにしてはどう？

A：あっ！　いつの間にか、ハネ出しが目的になっていました。付加価値を付けていない動きをできるだけ減らさなければいけなかったのに。

B：そうなんだ、これって、かなりの経験者でも、間違ってしまうことがあるんだよね。それで、両手スイッチをやめたら、彼女は、何秒空くのかな？

A：We have applied the auto-eject concept to the forming machine.

B：It's not bad, but something is lacking. Now, there is the remaining problem that she has to keep pushing two start-buttons with both left and right hands during the entire forming cycle.

A：But this is our safety standard, so it is hard to change.

B：But in this way, we cannot get the potential efficiency from auto-eject. She needs to be freed from the machine. You can choose infrared sensors or mechanical shutters for protection. Then, how about a limit switch instead of two buttons?

A：I see. We mistakably took auto-eject itself as our objective. Instead, we should eliminate non-value-creating elements as much as possible!

B：That's right! This is a common mistake even for experienced people. Anyway, how many seconds will she have, if you get rid of those both-hands buttons?

Chapter

4

工程の安定化
Process Stability

自工程品質保証
What is Zone Control ?

後工程が引き取るモノは「不良ゼロ」でなければならない

先に解説したジャスト・イン・タイムは、引き取る部品の中に不良が含まれているようでは、うまく動きません。ストア（店）に置かれた部品や仕掛品は「不良ゼロ」でなければならないのです。

不良品を後工程へ送らないのはかんばんのルール
かんばんのルールのうち5番目は、「不良品を絶対に後工程へ送らない」ということです。

自働化
自働化とは、問題や不良が発生したらいつでもただちに生産が自動的に止まるという意味です。（自働化という言葉が生まれる以前のことですが）豊田佐吉翁が1920年代に発明した自動織機は、自働化を具現化した最初の機械でした。

自工程品質保証とは
マネジメントの階層ごとに、彼または彼女の担当範囲（ゾーン）について深く考察することが推奨されます。理想の世界では、不良を決してつくらないことも可能かもしれませんが、不幸なことに、現実世界では、不良はいつでもどこでも発生する可能性があるものです。しかし、もし不良をつくってしまっても、それを次工程へ送らないようにすることはできます。これを、私たちは「自工程品質保証」と呼びます。自動停止機構は、これらの手法の1つでもあります。

The fifth of the six rules for Kanban
The fifth of the six rules for using kanban effectively is that defective parts are never sent to the next process.

Let's review Jidoka!
Jidoka means ensuring that a production process stops automatically and immediately whenever a problem or defect occurs. The earliest style of jidoka was invented by Mr. Sakichi Toyoda in the form of his automatic looms in the 1920's.

What is Zone Control?
Each management level should think of managing in terms of his or her "zone." In an ideal world, it might be possible to produce with no defects, but unfortunately accidental defects can occur everywhere at any time in the real world. However, even if we might make defects, we can stop them before they go to the next process. We call this "Zone Control". As an example, automatic line stop is one of the methods for Zone Control.

伝統的な検査による品質保証と、自工程品質保証

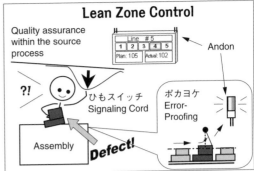

伝統的な検査による品質保証
伝統的な大量生産方式では、ものをつくっている工程とは違う部門に所属する専任の検査担当者が、品質のチェックを行ってきました。

リーンな自工程品質保証
リーンなモノづくりでは、つくったところですぐに問題を発見するために、製造工程の作業者に品質保証の権能を持たせ、工程内にポカヨケを付けます。

ポカヨケとは？
ポカはうっかりミス、ヨケは防止の意味。作業者が間違った部品を取り付けてしまったり、部品を取り付け忘れたり、逆向きに取り付けてしまう等々のミスを犯さないようにするための、シンプルで安価な機構のことです。

ポカヨケのタイプ
- 停止系：最も強力なポカヨケ。例えば、ワークが定位置に正しくセットされなければ始動しない。
- 警告系：ブザー（音）やライト（光）で何か異常があることを知らせるもの。

ポカヨケのポイント
- シンプル、丈夫で長持ちする
- 高信頼性
- 安価
- 現場にマッチしている

Traditional Inspection
In traditional mass production, a specialized inspector outside of the production process checked for quality.

Lean Zone Control
Lean producers assign quality assurance to operators and employ Error-Proofing devices within each production process in order to detect the problems at the sources.

What is "Poka-Yoke", or Error-Proofing?
"Poka" means inadvertent error, and "Yoke" means prevention. Poka-Yoke means implementing simple and inexpensive devices that help operators avoid mistakes in their work caused by the wrong parts, leaving out a part, installing a part backwards, etc.

The types of Error-Proofing
- Shutdown : They are the most powerful Error-Proofing devices. For example, a machine will not start if a work piece is set incorrectly.
- Warning : They alert us to something abnormal by a buzzer or light.

A good Error-Proofing :
- Simple, with long life and low maintenance
- High reliability
- Inexpensive
- Designed for the workplace situation.

定位置停止——Fixed-Position Stop System

トヨタの最終組立ラインで工夫されてきた「定位置停止」は、異常を検知したらその場で即座に停止するのではなく、決められた1サイクルの仕事が完了する位置までコンベヤが動いた後に停止する仕組みです。異常を検知してから定位置まで動く間に、問題を解決して復旧するのが一番ですが、それができない時は、コンベヤは定位置で停止し、次のサイクルが始まることはありません。

サイクル内の任意の場所で停止すると、問題工程以外の工程で部品の取付けミスなどを誘発する恐れがあります。1サイクル完了まで動いてから停止するのなら、ほかの工程へ品質上・安全上の悪影響を及ぼすことはありません。また、この方法によるのなら、問題があったら停止するという原理を大切にしつつも、停止時間を極小化することが可能になるでしょう。

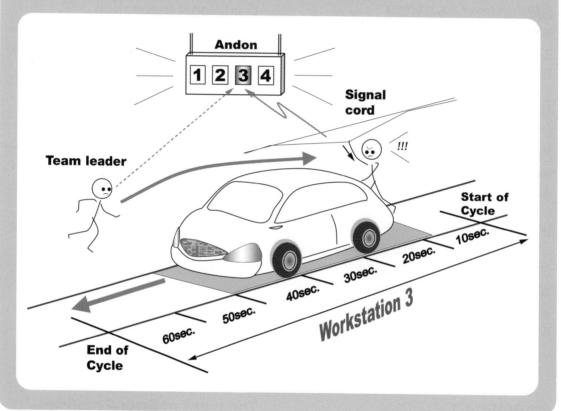

ポカヨケで何を検知するのか？——Three types of Poka-Yoke

①ワーク自体のバラツキ
Detecting deviations in the work piece.

②作業のやり方の間違い
Detecting operations not adhering to the standardized work.

Incorrect glue

③値のバラツキ
Detecting deviations from some predetermined value.

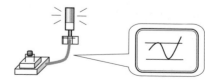

Error-Proofing for the number of holes　穴あけ工程のポカヨケ

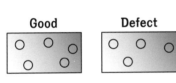

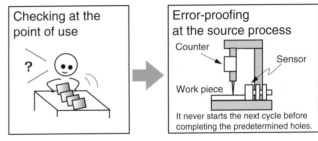

Let's talk　カウンターを使って加工数をチェックする

A： 今月は新製品を出しました。既存ラインでつくっています。

A： We launched the new product this month. We produce them with the current production resources.

B： 出来高がばらついているね。それに、総作業量に対して作業者が多くないかな？

B： The output of this line is fluctuating. And don't you have too many operators for the total work content?

A： この金属板の穴の数をチェックするために、作業者を追加する必要がありました。穴あけ漏れは5％で、まだ改善できていません。穴あけ点数不良のために、出来高もばらついてしまうのです。

A： We needed an additional operator to check the number of holes on this metal sheet. The rate of lack of holes is 5％ and we have not improved it yet. This causes the fluctuation of the output.

B： 使うところでチェックしていたら不良は減らない。源流、つまり穴あけ工程で不良をつくらせないようにした方が効果的だよ。

B： The defects cannot be reduced when you check them at the point of use. It is more effective to prevent operators from making defects at the source process, or the drilling.

A： 決められた数の穴を必ず加工するようにするには——穴あけ機にカウンターを付けるとよいかしら？

A： In order to drill the holes in the correct number ……, we can attach a counter to the drilling machine, can't we?

B： よいアイデアだね。生産技術がカウンターやセンサを持っていると思うよ。彼らに、ちょっと来てもらうことはできるかな？

B： It's a nice idea. Production Engineering might have the counters or sensors that you need. Could you ask them to come here now?

標準作業
What is Standardized Work ?

標準作業とは

トヨタ生産方式では、どのような業務においても、それが2回以上行われるのなら標準化すべきと、強く推奨されます。作業標準と標準作業の違いがわかるように説明することが大切です。

標準作業とは？

標準作業とは、現在の技術や製法を前提として、良い品質のものを、安全に、より安く、ムダなくつくるための作業の基準です。

標準作業の3要素

標準作業とは、製造工程の作業者1人ひとりについて、標準作業の3要素に基づく正しい作業方法を定め、定着させることです。
1. タクトタイム
2. 作業順序
3. 標準手持ち

繰返し作業であること

標準作業の作業要素は繰返し作業になっていなければいけません。サイクル外の作業は、流れ化を台なしにし、タクトタイムに合わせてムダなく安定してつくり続けることを不可能にしてしまうものです。これらは必要なものかもしれませんが、チームリーダーや水すましのようなサポートスタッフに担わせるべきです。

What is Standardized Work ?

Standardized Work is the basis of operations to make correct products in the safest, easiest and most effective way based on the current technologies and formulas.

Three elements of Standardized Work

Standardized Work means establishing precise procedures for each operator's work, based on three elements:
1. Takt time
2. Work sequence
3. Standard inventory (In-process stock)

Out-of-cycle Work

All work elements should be in cycle. Any out-of-cycle work destroys continuous flow and makes it difficult to maintain efficient and consistent production to takt time. These tasks may be needed, but they should be given to supporting members, such as team leaders or mizusumashi (material handlers).

Creating Standardized Work　標準作業をつくる

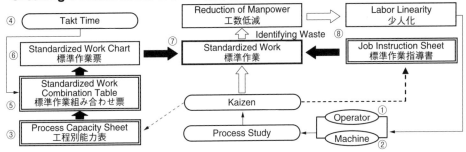

◇標準作業は何のため？——The Purpose of Standardized Work

改善に唯一最善の解というものは存在しません。管理監督者には、そこに働く人々の人間性を尊重し、ともに作業を設計すること、また現場改善を通して標準作業を継続的に改訂し続けることが求められます。

標準作業の目的は、継続的な改善の基盤をつくることにあります。これは、それぞれのシフトにおける今の作業のやり方を紙の上に描き出すことであり（表準作業）、作業のバラツキを減らすことになるはずです。また標準作業があれば、新人のトレーニングもやりやすく、ケガや過重な負荷を減らすことにもつながるでしょう。

The purpose of standardized work is to provide a basis for continuous improvement through kaizen. The benefits of standardized work include documentation of current process for all shifts, reductions in variability, easier training of new operators, and reductions in injuries and strain.

◇標準作業のつくり方——How to Create Standardized Work

標準作業は、次の3つのフォーム＋標準作業指導書（Job Instruction Sheet）で構成されます。

①工程別能力表
工程別能力表は、真の加工能力を確定し、ボトルネックを見つけてこれを改善するために、一連の加工工程における機械の能力を計算するために使います。

②標準作業組み合わせ票
標準作業組み合わせ票は、人の作業と歩行、機械の加工時間の組み合わせを、作業者ごとに順番に書き下すために使うものです。

③標準作業票
標準作業票は、設備と工程全体のレイアウトと関連付けて、作業者の動きとモノの配置を示すものです。

① Process Capacity Sheet
This is used to calculate the capacity of each machine in a set of processes in order to confirm true capacity and to identify and eliminate bottlenecks.

② Standardized Work Combination Table
This is used to describe the combination of manual work time, walk time, and machine processing time for each operator in a sequence.

③ Standardized Work Chart
This shows operator movement and material location in relation to the machine and overall process layout.

Process Study

ステップ1：まず、作業を要素に分解する

— What are the work elements for making one piece ? —

さて、作業分析です。しかし、いきなりストップウォッチで測ってはいけません。時間測定の前に、まず、1個をつくるのに本当に必要な作業とは何かをよく観察し、作業要素に分解します。作業を要素ごとに分解して観察し、測定することによってムダがよく見え、「廃除」できるようにもなるのです。

Example of Process Study

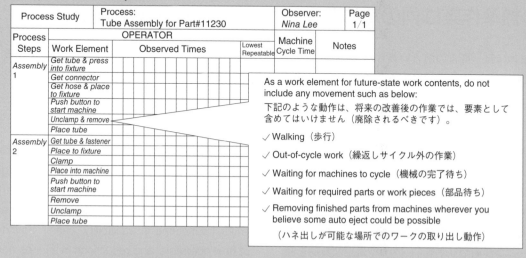

Process Study	Process: Tube Assembly for Part#11230				Observer: *Nina Lee*	Page 1/1
Process Steps	OPERATOR				Machine Cycle Time	Notes
	Work Element	Observed Times		Lowest Repeatable		
Assembly 1	*Get tube & press into fixture*					
	Get connector					
	Get hose & place to fixture					
	Push button to start machine					
	Unclamp & remove					
	Place tube					
Assembly 2	*Get tube & fastener*					
	Place to fixture					
	Clamp					
	Place into machine					
	Push button to start machine					
	Remove					
	Unclamp					
	Place tube					

As a work element for future-state work contents, do not include any movement such as below:
下記のような動作は、将来の改善後の作業では、要素として含めてはいけません（廃除されるべきです）。

√ Walking（歩行）

√ Out-of-cycle work（繰返しサイクル外の作業）

√ Waiting for machines to cycle（機械の完了待ち）

√ Waiting for required parts or work pieces（部品待ち）

√ Removing finished parts from machines wherever you believe some auto eject could be possible
（ハネ出しが可能な場所でのワークの取り出し動作）

ステップ2：作業時間を正しく測定し、個々の作業要素について本当に必要な時間を知る

— What is the actual time required for each work element ? —

- 現場で実際の時間を測定せよ。
- 作業者の手の動きがよく見える位置に立て。

- 作業要素ごとに測定せよ。
- それぞれの作業要素を、複数サイクルにわたって何度も測定せよ。
- 認定を得ている作業者を観察せよ。

- 人の時間と機械の時間を常に分けて扱うべし。

- それぞれの作業要素について、測定値の中で、最も速くかつ再現性のある時間を採用せよ（平均値ではなく）。
- 現場での礼儀を忘れるな。

- Collect real times at the process.
- Position yourself so you can see the operator's hand motions.
- Time each work element separately.
- Time several cycles of each work element.

- Observe an operator who is qualified to perform the job.
- Always separate operator time and machine time.
- Select the lowest repeatable time for each element (rather than an average time).

- Remember shop floor courtesy.

※ LEI のワークブック Creating Continuous Flow（June 2001）17〜25 ページより

How many operators do you need to meet Takt Time?
タクトタイムに合わせるのに必要な作業者は何人？

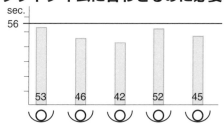

$$\text{The Number of Operators (作業者数)} = \frac{\text{Total Work Contents (総作業時間)}}{\text{Takt Time (タクトタイム)}}$$

$$= \frac{238 \text{ sec.}}{56 \text{ sec.}} = 4.25$$

Four operators are not sufficient, but five are too many.

Let's talk
必要な作業者は何人？

A： 前回の改善セッションで、すべての作業者の作業量をタクトタイム以下にすることができました。タクトタイム56秒に合わせて、出来高も安定しています。

A： At the last kaizen session, we made the work contents for each operator less than takt time. And the output is stable in accordance with the takt time, 56 seconds.

B： 総作業時間は238秒、今の作業者は5人だね。238秒をタクトタイムで割ると、必要な作業者数がわかるんだよ。

B： It takes 238 seconds for the total work contents and you have 5 operators now. Dividing 238 seconds by takt time, you can get the number of operators required here.

A： 4.25人必要ということですよね？ 5人では多過ぎる？

A： You mean that we need 4.25 operators, don't you? And 5 operators are too many…?

B： 一般的な話だけれど、この計算結果の端数が0.3未満なら、人を増やすべきではないんだよ。

B： Generally speaking, when the fraction of this calculation is less than 0.3, you should not add one more operator.

A： 各シフトで約30分、残業しなければならないわ。

A： In this case, we will need about 30 minutes of overtime work every shift.

B： 残業できない作業者の分は、君たちリーダーが埋めるんだ。そうしたら、もっと改善しなくちゃいけないって、切実にわかるだろう？

B： You team leaders will have to fill in for the operators who cannot do overtime. You will become aware of the necessity to do much more kaizen, won't you?

A： わかりました。やってみます。

A： Yes, we can do it!

目で見る管理
Visual Management
―How to manage visually

目で見る管理は改善の基盤

「目で見る管理」は、改善の重要な基盤であり、常に次のステージを目指して継続的に進化すべきものです。日本国内では今や説明不要と思われるほどですが、海外拠点では、その目的と手法を丁寧に説明することが必要でしょう。

目で見る管理とは？

目で見る管理とは、あらゆる治工具や部品、製造の動き、出来高や生産性を、わかりやすく表示することを意味します。こうすれば、関係する誰にでも、製造の状態がひと目でわかるようになります。

標準なくして管理なし

目で見る管理を私たちの現場で実現するには、まずわかりやすい標準を持たなければなりません。トヨタ生産方式では、標準とは、書棚の分厚い書類のことではありません。標準とは、かくあるべしという姿の、はっきりしたイメージです。

なぜ標準が大切なのか？

標準があるから異常がすぐにわかり、その対策をとることもできるのです。トヨタ生産方式においては、標準とは行動と結び付いたものでなければなりません。

よい標準とは？

シンプルで明確、視覚的であるべきです。また、標準は常に改善され続けなければなりません。

What is visual management ?

It means the placement in plain view of all tools, parts, production activities and indicators of production system performance. Then the status of the system can be understood at a glance by everyone involved.

Standards are the basis of visual management.

To achieve visual worksite management, start with setting easy-to-understand standards. In the Toyota Production System, "standards" does not mean thick files on the shelves. A standard should be a clear image of a desired condition.

Why are standards so important ?

Standards make abnormalities immediately obvious so that corrective action can be taken. In the Toyota Production System, standards should be linked to action.

What makes a standard effective ?

A good standard is simple, clear and visual. And it is always improved.

Basic items to be made visual at our workplace

⑥Job Instruction for each operator

①Location and Line Name
(Where are we?)

⑦Planned vs. Actual Output
(Production Analysis Board)
It shows the performance of the line, cell or process on an hourly basis with planned versus actual production. When production does not correspond to the plan, the problem is recorded and a cause is sought.

C-01
Line #1

Type
A/B/C/D

42 sec.

Layout

②Part#
(What do we produce?)

③Takt Time

④Layout and Flow
⑤Work Distribution

Finished Goods

Each workstation or work area should be defined clearly.

◇まずは目で見る管理の基本
—— Basic items to make visual at the workplace

それでは、現場で見えるようにすべきものとは、何でしょう？　「すべてが見える」のが理想ですが、まずは最低限、次の項目は必須です。これらが見えるようになっていないなら、すぐに表示しましょう。

①ここはどこ？
ここがどこなのか、誰でもわかるように、製造ラインやストアの所番地と名前を表示します。

②何をつくっているのか？　何を置いているのか？
製造ラインであれば、何をつくっているのかわかるように表示します。ストアであれば、何を置く場所かがわかるように表示します。
例えば、
・品番A〜Dの組立
・成形完了部品

③タクトタイム
顧客が求めるペース。定時稼働時間を顧客要求数で割ったもの。

④レイアウトとモノの流れ

⑤作業者の編成
⑥作業内容の指示
⑦計画と出来高（生産管理板）
計画と出来高は、時間単位でわかるようにしましょう。日次では、生産をうまくコントロールするには不十分です。

① The location address and name
The name and address of each production line (or store) should be displayed clearly so everyone knows where he or she is.

② Assigned Products / Stored Materials
In a production line, the name of products produced should be displayed. In a supermarket, the type of materials stored should be displayed. For example：
・Assembly of Part Number A,B,C and D
・Store：Molded Parts

③ Takt Time
The pace required by the customer：the available production time divided by the customer demand.

④ Layout and flow of operators, machines and materials

⑤ Work distribution
⑥ Job instruction
⑦ Planned vs. actual output (Production Analysis Board)
Planned versus actual production output should be made visual on an hourly basis. A daily-basis indication is inadequate to control production effectively.

表示を見るのではなく、モノや動きで異常がわかることが大切

It is more effective for you to identify abnormalities through seeing operators' movement, machines, work pieces and materials themselves, rather than reading charts and descriptions. At the same time, you will be freed from making burdensome charts!

Example of a Visualized Parts Presentation

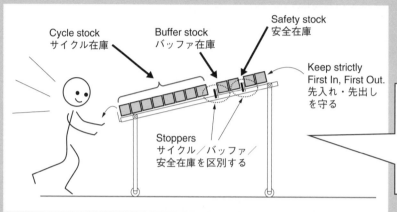

Cycle stock
サイクル在庫

Buffer stock
バッファ在庫

Safety stock
安全在庫

Keep strictly
First In, First Out.
先入れ・先出し
を守る

Stoppers
サイクル／バッファ／
安全在庫を区別する

Instead of counting containers, we can see at a glance if it is the normal condition or not. In addition to the visibility, we can maintain FIFO quite easily with a flow rack.

Example of a Defects Presentation

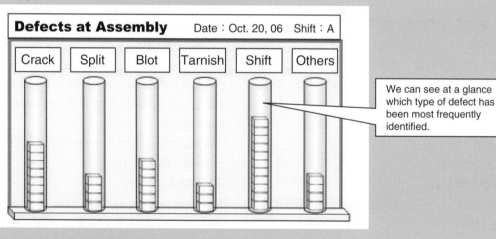

Defects at Assembly Date：Oct. 20, 06 Shift：A

| Crack | Split | Blot | Tarnish | Shift | Others |

We can see at a glance which type of defect has been most frequently identified.

役立つ豆知識

—— Defining Pack-Out-Qty. is the first step to Parts Visualization.

部品の見える化の第1歩は、各部品の入り数（収容数）を決めることから始まります。最終製品の入り数の倍数または約数とするのがよいでしょう。「数える」作業を大幅に減らすことができ、正しい数量が保たれているか、トレーの数でわかるようになります。

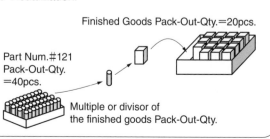

Finished Goods Pack-Out-Qty.＝20pcs.

Part Num.#121
Pack-Out-Qty.
＝40pcs.

Multiple or divisor of
the finished goods Pack-Out-Qty.

Making things visible must be linked to immediate corrective action!

Tester

Production Analysis Board					Date : Jul. 21, 06
Assembly Line＃01				Leader : Audrey Keane	
Required Q'ty : 775 pcs./Shift				Takt Time : 36 sec./p	
Time	Hourly		Cumulative		Problems /Causes
	Planned	Actual	Planned	Actual	
08：00-09：00	100	100	100	100	
09：00-09：45	75	75	175	175	
10：00-11：00	100	60	275	235	Probe Broke
11：00-12：00	100	62	375	297	Unsolved
13：00-14：00	100	61	475	359	Unsolved

You should take countermeasures against problems immediately !

Let's talk　即座に対策を講じるべし！

A： 生産管理板をつくりました。時間単位の計画と実績が、誰にでもわかります。

A： We made this Production Analysis Board. Everybody can see the planned quantity versus the actual output on an hourly basis.

B： う〜ん。生産管理板自体は悪くないんだけど、何かおかしいところがあると思わない？

B： Um…The Board itself is not wrong, but there is something incorrect. Don't you think so?

A： おかしいところ……？

A： Something incorrect……?

B： 時間当たり100個必要なんだよね？　10時から11時には、60個しかできなかった。

B： You need 100 pieces per hour, don't you? Between 10 and 11 o'clock, you had produced only 60 pieces.

A： はい。それは管理板からわかります。検査機の2つのプローブのうち、1つが壊れたのです。

A： Yes, we can see it from the Board. One of two probes of the tester broke.

B： 続く11時から12時も62個。今、午後2時だよね。3時間以上、問題を放っておいたわけだ。

B： Then, between 11 and 12 o'clock, 62 pieces. It is 2:00 p.m. now. You have left problems unsolved for more than three hours!

A： ラインリーダーには修理はできません。

A： But, Line Leaders cannot repair the tester.

B： しょっちゅう壊れるなら、当面は交換用のプローブを準備しておいて、壊れたらすぐにラインリーダーが交換しなければいけない。それから、真因の解決も忘れずにね。

B： If it breaks so frequently, you must have some replacement-probes for a time and Line Leaders are required to change the broken probe immediately whenever it breaks. In addition, don't forget to resolve the root-cause!

Chapter

5

改善に終わりなし
The Lean Journey

限量経営 ──人と設備──

Genryou Management
─Labor Linearity and Capital Linearity─

「限られた量」の人・モノ・金で安くつくって儲けること
──Constraints in resources to meet business needs is the mother of the Toyota Way.

限量経営とは、限られた量の人・モノ・金で製品を安くつくり、売上げが伸びる時も伸びない時も利益を出す、という考え方と動き方を表した故・大野耐一氏の言葉です。今日のイメージからは想像し難いのですが、トヨタ自動車の歴史を学んだことのある人なら、「金がなかった」というフレーズが頻繁に登場することをご存知でしょう。大正年間に繊維産業で一時代を築いた豊田グループでしたが、であればこそと言うべきか、第2次大戦敗戦後、欧米に比べて格段に小さな国内市場、乏しい資金という環境の下、日本の自動車メーカーとしていかに生き抜くか、という強い危機感と高い目標を持っていたと伝えられます。

ところで今日、明治・大正・昭和の日本の歩みを背景に「限量」を説明するのは、なかなか難しくなっています。対日感情がそれぞれに異なるのは従前通りですが、各国の新世代の人々との認識ギャップも無視できません。例えば皆さんは、日本の近現代に関する知識がほとんどない世代や集団に、各国各地で頻繁に出会っていることでしょう（あるいは日本国内でも）。一方、先進国であれ途上国であれ、資本の自由化によって「金がなければ市場で調達」ということが、普通に行われるようになりました。このような環境にあっては、歴史的な背景を伝えながらも、「限量」の意味を、より具体的、理論的に説明する必要があると思われるのです。うっかりすると、「リソースに限界があるのは当然ではないですか？」と質問されてしまいそうです。

前置きが長くなりました。ここでは、大野耐一氏の「限量経営」において、わけても特徴的な人の限量＝「少人化」と、モノと金（マシン＆投資）の限量＝「段階的設備投資」を紹介します。もう1つの限量である、モノと金（＝部材調達）の限量＝「後工程引き取り」は、Chapter 2を参照してください。

焦土からの出発（1945～1956）
第2次世界大戦の敗北により、壊滅的な打撃を受けた戦後の日本経済には、わずかな資本しかなかった。当時、日本の産業が生き残る唯一の道は、アメリカ流の大量生産とは違うやり方を見つけ出すことだけだったのだ。当然ながら、豊田グループもまた事業資金不足に直面していた。

Devastated War-Torn Japan, 1945-1956

The devastated war-torn Japanese economy in the post-WWII period had little capital. The only ticket for survival in those days for Japanese industries was to find some alternative ways to the American way of mass production. Of course, the Toyoda Group also faced this shortage of funds.

"Genryou Management", or the Linearity of Labor, Material and Capital.
限量経営とは、「売れ」に合わせて安くつくり、売上増でも売上減でも、必ず利益を出すこと

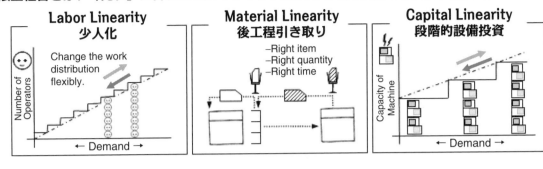

限量経営とは？ ·····
大野耐一氏の教えの１つ。限られた経営資源で安くモノをつくり、売上増でも売上減でも利益を出すという考え方と方法の体系（日本語で、"ゲン"は「限られた」、"リョウ"は「分量」という意味）。

What is Genryou Management?
Genryou Management is a precept preached by Mr. Taiichi Ohno. It is a framework to make profits during periods of both growth and decline in sales through making products at lower costs with limited resources. ("Gen" means "limited" and "ryou" means "amount" in Japanese.)

少人化 ·····
需要の増減に合わせて作業者数を増やしたり減らしたりできるよう、作業者の配置を柔軟にするという考え方。
これにより、需要の変化に対する単位生産当たりの作業者の人数を、かなりの程度で、線形化することができる。
遺憾ながら、需要減のときにラインの人数を減らすということが、私たちにはなかなかできないのだった。

Shoujinka, Labor Linearity
A philosophy for flexibly manning a production process so that the number of operators increases or decreases as the demand changes. This gives the process the approximate linearity of the amount of labor per unit (or part) produced as the demand changes.
Regrettably, we often fail to reduce adequately the number of operators from the line when demand declines.

段階的設備投資 ·····
需要の変化に対して設備能力を少しずつ増やしたり除却したりできるよう、設備を小さな能力の単位で構想し、調達するという考え方。
これにより、単位生産当たりの設備投資額を、ほとんど線形にすることができる。
遺憾ながら私たちは、初期段階で能力が過大な設備を構想してしまうという失敗を繰り返してきた。

Capital Linearity, incremental investment
A philosophy for designing and purchasing machinery so that small amounts of capacity can be added or subtracted as demand changes.
This gives the plant the approximate linearity of the amount of capital needed per unit (or part).
Regrettably, we continue to design machines to have too much capacity in the initial stages.

なぜ段階的設備投資が有利なのか？

—— Advantage of Capital Linearity over Large-scale Investment

Assumption〔前提条件〕

You need to build up a capacity of 100,000 units of annual output. You have two options：
100,000台/年の能力増強が必要。道は2つ：

Option A　　　　　　　　　　**Option B**

Large-scale Model
大量生産モデル

100,000
units/year

It tends to be large, high-volume, multi-functional and accordingly expensive.

Linear Model
段階的設備投資モデル

10,000
units/year

×**10**sets

Cell type layout

It should simply meet estimated takt time requirements and should be small.

Actual Demand		
Beyond 100,000 units	If you get another new set of machines, the capital investment per unit would be significantly high.	You can add the lines as required with each 10,000 units of capacity.
Less than 100,000 units	It will be almost impossible to decrease capacity and keep efficiency at the current level.	You can subtract capacity by shutting down as many lines as required.

Capital Investment /unit

100,000 units　　200,000 units

+10,000 units

Almost Irreversible!
ほぼ不可逆。能力を小さく
することはできない。

Demand/year

 役立つ豆知識

流れの中で使える設備 —— Right-Sized Tools

流れの中で使える設備がカタログには載っていないという事情は、どの国でも同じですね。下記のキーワードを参考に、洗浄機など、比較的簡単なものから、実際につくってみることをお勧めします。

- ・必要な能力がある
- ・メンテナンスが容易で、可動率が高い

- ・段取り替えが素早い
- ・移設が容易
- ・小さな単位で能力増強が可能な設計

- highly capable
- easy to maintain and available to produce whenever needed

- quick to changeover
- easy to move
- designed to be installed in small increments of capacity

How do you design and lay out your machines? 構想段階から設備を変えよう！

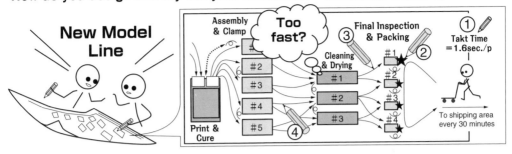

Let's talk　いつでもどこでも「整流」を目指すべし！

A： これが今度の新製品の製造ラインの構想図です。リーンの考え方をちょっと採り入れたつもりです。必要数は月に100万個、3シフトで20日稼働として、タクトタイムは1.6秒に1個です。

B： なるほど、工程がちょっとは連結されてるね。えーっと…このレイアウト図上で、最終製品が完成する場所に印を付けてみて？

A： ここと、ここと… 4カ所。最終工程は、検査機と梱包です。

B： その前は？ どこから来るの？ 何カ所あるかな？ 検査・梱包から前工程まで、それぞれ線でつないでみて。

A： えーとですね、レイアウト図では、前工程の洗浄・乾燥機が…3台。…あれ？ なぜ3台にしちゃったんだろう？ 4台で検査・梱包と直結した方がよかったのに…。

B： ああ、洗浄・乾燥機1台当たりの能力が大き過ぎるからだよ。単純に必要数を能力で割れば3台だよね。どうすればよいと思う？

A： This is our draft of new-model production lines. We intend to bring in some lean concepts. We need to produce one million pieces every month, so assuming 20 operating days every month with three shifts, takt time is 1.6 second per piece.

B： I can see that some of the processes are connected. Well, on this chart, mark up all of the final processes where finished goods are completed.

A： One, two, ——there are four points. The final process is inspection and packing.

B： Where does each work piece come from? How many sources are there? Line up from each inspection-packing process to its source.

A： Let's see. On our drawing, we have three cleaning-drying machines upstream. Hmm, why did we set three? We should set four cleaning-drying machines and connect them directly to each tester.

B： Ah, I see. Because its capacity is too much, you got the result "three", simply dividing the demand by its capacity. What can you do here?

全員参加 —実践会、創意くふう提案制度—

Employee Involvement
—Practical Kaizen Training & Suggestion Programs—

人の力を引き出そう! —— Why Employee Involvement ?

全員を改善活動に巻き込む

お客様が求めるものを、求めるときに、求める量だけ提供することができる流れをつくりたいと願うなら、会社の内外を貫く流れに関係するすべての人々に、自ら進んで働き方を変えてもらわなければなりません。時期の違いや関与の深い浅いはあっても、全員を巻き込むことが不可欠です。

指示に従うだけではもったいない

人間はとてもフレキシブルで、大きな能力を持っています。ひとたびトヨタ生産方式の考え方を知り、基本的な手法を身に付けたなら、自ら改善に貢献したいと考えるようになるはずです。

力を結集するには

トヨタ生産方式に学び、改革を進めようという活動は、トップダウンで始まるものかもしれません。しかし、改革は1人でできるものではなく、また、上から指示しただけでうまく動くものでもありません。そこで、人々の能力を引き出し、力を結集することが大切になるのです。いわゆる方針展開とともに、人々の能力を引き出すための実践的な教育訓練や改善サークル、改善提案制度が欠かせないのです。

What is Employee Involvement?

If you are eager to realize a production flow that can provide the right item at the right time in the right quantity as required by your customers, you should motivate everyone connected to the flow to want to change for themselves the way they do their work. Their involvement is crucial to your success, even though there may be differences in the amount of time it takes and the level of their engagement.

People's Latent Potential

People are very flexible and have great abilities. Once they have gotten the way of thinking and trained themselves in the basic arts of TPS, most of them will be willing to contribute something to kaizen.

How to Concentrate People's Efforts

A lean conversion may be started as a top-down process in many companies. However, nobody can realize it by him/herself and any new system cannot run well only by orders from above. Therefore, both enhancing people's abilities and directing them appropriately are absolutely necessary. Practical kaizen training programs, kaizen circle activities and suggestion programs are needed together with policy deployment.

Enhance people's ability through practical programs to support Policy Deployment.

方針展開に沿った実践的なプログラムで、
働く人の能力を引き出そう！

- **Kaizen Workshops**　　実践会
- **Kaizen Circle Activities**　改善サークル活動
- **Suggestion Programs**　提案制度

Suggestions

よい品 よい考
Good Product, Good Thinking

Kaizen Activity

実践会で学ぶ

教室での座学は、もちろんある程度は必要ですが、改善は実践を通して学ぶものです。
実践会では、自分の職場の改善テーマと改善の方法を自分たちで決めるところから始めて、限られた時間内で実践し、成果をまとめて発表することで、改善を学ぶことができます。また、次の改善テーマを見つけ出すよい機会ともなるでしょう。

Learning to do kaizen through kaizen workshops

Of course we need some study in classrooms, but kaizen is to be learned through actual practice.

You can really learn to do Kaizen in practical Kaizen workshops, starting with setting your own targets and selecting methods, practicing them at your workplace in a set period of time, and making a presentation. It will also be a good opportunity to find out your next challenges.

改善サークル活動

小集団活動は、日本的な手法として最も有名なものかもしれませんが、単に小集団をつくっただけでは、うまく動きません。グループは方針展開に沿った明確な目標を持ち、管理者は彼らを正しくサポートしなければなりません。数字よりも、活動を通してメンバーの能力を高めることが大切です。

Kaizen Circle Activities

Small group activity may be the most famous method of the Japanese way of management, but it will not work automatically just by setting up groups. Groups should have clear goals under your policy deployment and managers should carefully support them. It is more important to enhance team-members'ability than to chase metrics.

創意くふう提案制度

トヨタの工場を見学すると、「よい品 よい考」と書かれた大きな横断幕が頭上に掲げられているのに気づくでしょう。トヨタは、「創意くふう提案制度」を1951年に始め、今も多くの提案が従業員から寄せられています。改善提案制度は、人々を改善活動に巻き込むのに、大きな力となるはずです。

Suggestion Programs

You can see large banners saying "Good Product, Good Thinking" overhead in any Toyota plant. Toyota started their suggestion program named "Sou-i Kufuh Tei-an Se-i-do" in 1951 and Toyota employees still contribute suggestions through this program. A suggestion program can be a great way to involve workers in your lean conversion.

活動管理板をつくろう！
倦まず弛まず改善を続けるべし
—A well-used Project Tracking Board can bring a continuous kaizen culture in your workplace!

いわゆる活動管理板。「見せる化」になってしまうと困りものですが、そこで働く人々に現状を理解してもらい、協力してもらうのに、大きな力となるでしょう。この種の活動管理板がなければ、つくりましょう。

Just to "make things visual" is not your true objective, but a project tracking board will stand by you to encourage every employee to understand the situation and contribute to the improvement activity. If you do not have this type of board yet, you should make one right away!

Example of the Project Tracking Board

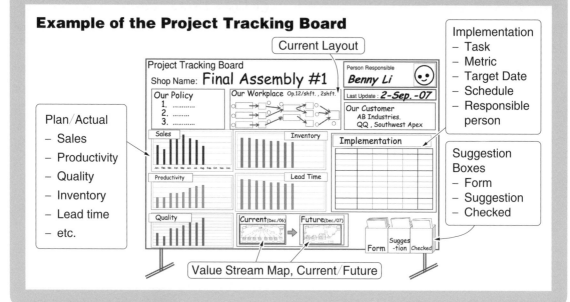

実践会は、どう進める？ —— How to promote the kaizen workshop

５日間の実践トレーニングがよく知られていますが、週に１回あるいは２週間に１回の社内実践会も効果的です。対象の職場、目標、実践、発表と評価、次の課題の発見について、管理者はきちんとサポートしなければなりません。

The five-day kaizen workshop may be more famous, but it is also effective to hold an one-day kaizen workshop every week or fortnightly. Managers should fully support the process by selecting the target workplaces, setting goals, implementing, presentation and evaluation, and identifying next challenges.

12th Kaizen Workshop
05-Sep.-07

- Time Table
  10:00- Opening session
  10:30- Practice
  16:00- Closing session
- Workplaces
  Final Assembly #1 - #4
  Shipping Dept.

The process should become "bottom-top-bottom".

What do we know?
What is the problem?
Why are we talking about it?
What are we doing about it?

キャッチボールを
繰り返すべし

改善は私が！

Manager

Team leaders

Let's talk　　自ら考え、実行するチームをつくろう！

A：毎月実践会を開催していますが、表面的で、ときどき後戻りしてしまうんです。

A：We hold a kaizen workshop once a month, but I am afraid they might not be substantive enough because sometimes things revert back to the old way after awhile.

B：もっと詳しく話してくれますか？　前回は何をしたの？　どんな改善をやったのか、具体的に教えてください。

B：Can you be more specific? What did you do last time? Exactly what kaizen did you do?

A：設備を移動して直線ラインを変形U字ラインにしたんです。でも、改善チームは何をすべきかをなかなか決められなくて、結局、私が言ってしまったんです。それで、今は改善が後戻りしています。

A：We moved equipment from a straight line to a modified U-shape. But, the team had much trouble deciding what to do, so finally I had to tell them.   And now the improvements are already regressing.

B：なるほど。君が「これをやりなさい」と言ってしまったんだね。どうして彼らが自分でよいアイデアにたどり着くようにもっていけなかったのかな？

B：I see. So, you told them what to do. Why couldn't you get them to come up with their own good ideas?

A：彼らはまだ原理原則がわかっていないようなんです。私が答えを言わなければ、彼らは間違ったことをしてしまったでしょう。あるいは、試行錯誤を通して正しい解を得ようとすれば、もっと時間がかかっていたと思います。

A：They still don't seem to get some basic concepts. If I didn't tell them the answer, they would've made a mistake. Or it would take a long time for them to find the right answer through trial & error.

B：しかしね、それをやらなくちゃいけないんだ。君は、１個流しをやってリードタイムを短縮してもらいたかったんだよね？　後戻りしてしまうのはなぜなのか、なぜ彼らが１個流しをやれないのか、君がもっとよく考えなくてはいけないよ。

B：Still, you have to try. You wanted them to use one piece flow to shorten the lead time, right? Think more about <u>why</u> they revert to the old way. Why <u>can't</u> they implement one piece flow??

5

改善に終わりなし ── 3
The Lean Journey

わたしたちの改善

Develop
Your Own Kaizen Guidelines!

Let's build a continuous improvement process within your team!

さらなる改善を！

1つ改善ができたら、その現場をもう一度よく見ましょう。人の手待ち、工程間の仕掛り、工程がつながっていないといった問題がまだあることに気づくはずです。次は、何をしたらよいでしょう？あなたにはもうそれがわかっているし、きっと実現できるはずです。

改善し続ける仕組みを築く

常にムダを探し、すぐに「廃除する」という意識と行動規範を、職場の人々が持たなければ、どのような改善も後退してしまいます。難しいと感じるかもしれませんが、ひとたび改善の意義を実感したなら、人々は、よりよい仕事のやり方を自ら追求するようになるでしょう。管理者は、彼らをていねいにサポートしなければなりません。

継続的改善が人を育てる

自ら現場を見て問題を発見し、自ら考えて改善を実践する、というサイクルを繰り返すことが、改善を理解し、力をつけるためのかけがえのない訓練の場となるのです。

Self-Reflection and Further Improvement

After implementing kaizen at your workplace, you should carefully observe it again. You can probably still see people waiting, work pieces stagnating between processes, some processes isolated, and the rest. What do you do next? You already know what the problem is and what needs to be done. This is your chance to try some new ideas.

Building Kaizen into Your Team

If people at your workplace don't have the mind-sets and behaviors to always try to identify and eliminate wastes immediately, any kaizen will regress. You might find it difficult, but once people have really understood the significance of kaizen, then they will be willing to pursue a better way of working by themselves. Managers need to support them with patience.

Developing People's Ability through Continuous Improvement

The process of the continuous improvement (CI) cycle of seeing the workplace, identifying problems and implementing solutions figured out by yourselves, can be an invaluable opportunity to understand kaizen and develop your ability.

Building your <u>own</u> continuous improvement process is essential to realize a successful lean transformation!

継続的改善を、仕事の中に埋め込むべし！

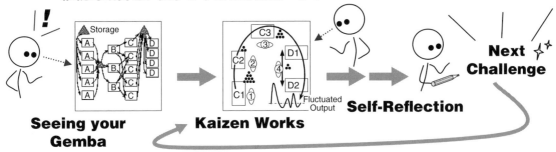

Seeing your Gemba → **Kaizen Works** → **Self-Reflection** → **Next Challenge**

自分の改善ガイドラインを持とう！

誰かに言われてやる改善ではなく、自分たちのものとして改善を考えることが大切です。このために、まず、自分たちの改善ガイドラインをつくってみるとよいでしょう。

Develop Your Own Kaizen Guidelines!

Instead of kaizen directed by someone else, you must personally understand it as your own process. An important step to gain a sense of kaizen ownership: you should develop your own kaizen guidelines by yourself!

どんなガイドライン？

トヨタ生産方式の本は、書店にいくらでもありますね。同じようなものをつくろうとするのは時間のムダというものかもしれません。しかし、あなたの現場で、あなたが実際にやった改善をもとに、毎日の仕事に役立つ指針をつくるのなら、それはたいへん意義深いことです。ここでは、美しく整った教科書を追求してもあまり意味はないでしょう。

What Kind of Guideline Do You Develop?

There are plenty of TPS books in the bookstores. It might be just a waste of time these days to create yet another similar one. But, it could be very helpful for you to create guidelines based on your own achievements at the workplace to really help your everyday work. Then it may not be so useful to seek some sort of sophisticated textbook.

どこから始める？

あなたはすでに、ライン改善の経験も、後工程引き取りの経験もあるはずです。あなたがたどった道を振り返って書き出してみましょう。

Where Do We Start?

Begin with your own experiences, such as improving production lines or establishing supermarkets with pull systems. Start by retracing and describing the route you took.

誰のために？

ガイドラインをつくるとき、それはあなたの職場の仲間のため、あなたの後に続く人のためであること、そしてなにより、あなた自身が自分の改善を振り返り、より深く問題を理解するためのものであることをいつも忘れないで下さい。

Who Will Use Your Guidelines?

In developing the guidelines, please remember that it is to be for your colleagues, for your successors, and especially for yourself to reflect on your kaizen experience and to understand even more deeply the problems you have overcome.

組立ラインの改善ガイドラインをつくってみよう！

—— Making Your Kaizen Guideline to Improve Assembly Lines

- **Make it simple and easy to understand with illustrations.**（わかりやすく）
- **Standardize as much as possible.**（常に標準化を目指すべし）

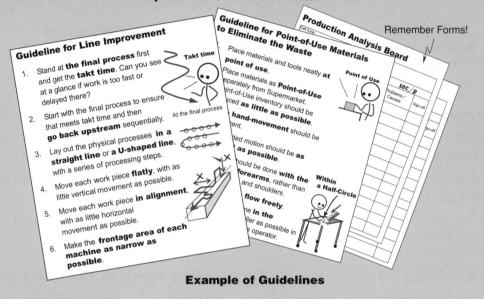

Guideline for Line Improvement

1. Stand at **the final process** first and get the **takt time**. Can you see at a glance if work is too fast or delayed there?

2. Start with the final process to ensure that meets takt time and then **go back upstream** sequentially.

3. Lay out the physical processes **in a straight line** or **a U-shaped line**, with a series of processing steps.

4. Move each work piece **flatly**, with as little vertical movement as possible.

5. Move each work piece **in alignment**, with as little horizontal movement as possible.

6. Make the **frontage area of each machine as narrow as possible**.

Guideline for Point-of-Use Materials to Eliminate the Waste

Place materials and tools neatly at point of use.

Place materials as Point-of-Use separately from Supermarket.

int-of-Use inventory should be ced **as little as possible**.

hand-movement should be nt.

ded motion should be as as possible.

ould be done with the forearms, rather than and shoulders.

flow freely.

e in the er as possible in the operator.

Takt time

At the final process

Point of Use

Within a Half-Circle

Remember Forms!

Production Analysis Board

Example of Guidelines

「何か質問はありますか？」から一歩も二歩も踏み出そう！

—— **Beyond just asking "Any Questions?"**

職場では、改善に関することのみならず、いろいろなことが毎日「説明」されているはずです。大切なことを説明した後で、「何か質問はありますか？」と聞いていませんか？　そして、人々は「いいえ、質問はありません」と繰り返しているのでは？　これでは、本当に伝わったかどうか、わかったものではありません。では、どうしたらよいのでしょう？　たとえば「今の説明から、あなたがわかったことを教えて下さい」と質問してみたらどうでしょう？　常に双方向のコミュニケーションを心がけましょう！

We often must explain many things related not only to kaizen but to other important issues (like safety, engineering process changes or QC procedures for new models). Do you ask "Any Questions?" after explaining something important and people respond just saying "No, we don't."? This is far from the most effective instruction. What questions might be more effective here? How about asking "please let me know what you've learned about this issue from my explanation."? Always look for interactive communication!

Any Questions?

No problem, But ???

Respecting People is Always the Basis of Your Kaizen.
人を尊重することが改善の基盤

How do we change from "Command" to "Commitment" ?
命令から約束へ

From Boss-and-Subordinates to "Team Members".
肩書きではなく、
ともに働く仲間として語り合おう

Confidence & Empathy

Esteem His/Her Valuable Time.
ともに働く人の時間を大切に

Let's talk 　一番よくわかっている人に教えてもらおう！

A ： 外観不良のキズが減らなくて困っています。

A : We are currently in trouble with cosmetic defects : scratches.

B ： なるほど、パレート図もあるし、傾向も把握してるね。確か、メアリーが外観検査担当だよね？　彼女の意見をよく聞いている？

B : Let me see…, Oh, I can see the trend from this Pareto chart. …Hmm. The Appearance Inspector is Mary, right? Have you heard her out and asked what she knows?

A ： えーとですね…、不良があったら報告を受けていますが、メアリーの考えをきちんと聞いたことはありませんでした。

A : Um… I receive a report when each defect occurs, …but I just realized that I had never asked her exactly.

B ： それじゃ、まず、メアリーに教えて下さいって頼んでみようか！

B : Well, let's ask her for help first!

A ： メアリー、おはよう！

A : Hi, Mary! Good morning! How are you?

M ： おはよう！　今日はどんな話？

M : Good morning! What's up today?

A ： メアリー、キズ不良について、気がついていることを教えてくれないかな？

A : Mary, please tell us what you think about the scratch defects.

M ： キズね。今も１つあったわ。リーダーには言ったんだけど、カシメ機でキズが起きるような気がしてる。でも、どのヘッドが悪いかはわからないの。まとめて箱に入って出てくるでしょ。で、順番がバラバラになっちゃうから…。

M : Scratches? I found one just now. As I've told the Team Leader, I think it might occur at the crimper. But, we can't identify which crimp-head made it. Parts are ejected into a batch box, so the sequence is not kept there.

A ： ありがとう、メアリー！　知らなかったよ。今まできちんと君の話を聞かなくてごめんなさい。

A : Thanks, Mary! I didn't know that. I'm sorry I didn't ask you sooner.

M ： え？　知らなかったの？　不良のことなら、もっと言わなきゃいけないことがあるわよ！

M : Really? Didn't you know that?! I have much more I can tell you about our defects!

付録 -1
Appendix-1

改善フォーム集
Forms

Production Analysis Board 　生産管理板

Line/Cell Name:	Team Leader:	Date:
Quantity Required:	**Takt Time:**	**Shift:**
		Num of operator:

Time	Hourly Plan / Actual	Cumulative Plan / Actual	Problem/Causes	Sign-off
： ～ ：	/	/		
： ～ ：	/	/		
： ～ ：	/	/		
： ～ ：	/	/		
： ～ ：	/	/		
： ～ ：	/	/		
： ～ ：	/	/		
： ～ ：	/	/		
： ～ ：	/	/		
： ～ ：	/	/		
： ～ ：	/	/		
： ～ ：	/	/		
： ～ ：	/	/		
： ～ ：	/	/		
： ～ ：	/	/		

Kaizen Express

Example of Production Analysis Board (生産管理板の例)

Production Analysis Board is a display that must be located at the exit of the cell(or the line), to show actual performance compared with planned performance on hourly basis.

生産管理板とは、時間単位に出来高の計画と実績を表示する掲示板です。セルまたはラインの出口に必ず設置しましょう。

Supervisor signs hourly.

Production Analysis Board

Line/Cell Name: Final Assembly #7		Team Leader: Benny Li		Date: April 07	
Quantity Required: 690p		Takt Time: 40sec./p		Shift: A	
				Num of operator: 16	

Time	Hourly Plan/Actual	Cumulative Plan/Actual	Problem/Causes	Sign-off
06:00~07:00	90 / 90	90 / 90		Sharon
07:00~08:00	90 / 88	180 / 178	Tester Minor Stoppage	Sharon
08:00~09:00	90 / 90	270 / 268		Sharon
09:10~10:10	90 / 85	360 / 353	Defects (Appearance)	Sharon
10:10~11:10	90 / 90	450 / 443		Roy
11:40~12:40	90 / 90	540 / 533		Sharon
12:40~13:40	90 / 86	630 / 619	Defects (Bad Parts)	Sharon
13:50~14:30	60 / 60	690 / 679		Sharon
O.T.	11 / 11	690 / 690		Roy

Remember Breaks

Area Manager signs at lunch and end of shift.

Just keeping visibility is not our real objective. Problems must be linked to corrective action!

Kaizen Express

Process Study Sheet (作業分析シート)

Process Study	Process:	Product:	Observer:	Date/Time:	Page /
Process Steps	Work Element	OPERATOR Observed Times 1 2 3 4 5 6 7 8 9 10	Repeatable	MACHINE Cycle Time	Notes

Kaizen Express

Example of Process Study Sheet (作業分析の例)

Process Study	Process: Final Assembly #7	Product: DV-020332	Observer: Benny	Date/Time: April 18, 2007 14:00	Page: 1/3

Process Steps	Work Element	1	2	3	4	5	6	7	8	9	10	Repeatable	MACHINE Cycle Time	Notes
		Observed Times												
Assembly 1	Get base & put into fixture	4	5	6	3	4	4	4	4	5	4	4		Base far away
	Get pin & put into fixture	6	8	10	15	9	10	10	7	11	10	10		Fixture unstable
	Put fixture into machine	2	2	1	2	2	3	2				2		
	Machine cycle	1	1	1								1	6	Operator waiting
	Remove	2	2	2	1	2	2					2		
	Check appearance & place	8	11	8	20	7	8	9	9	8		8		Checking unstable
	Subtotal											27		
Assembly 2	Get lower case													
	Get work piece													
	Put into lower cas...													Insertion unstable
	Get upper case &													
	Put into forming n...													Machine gate far away
	...													
	...													

Timing Tips
- Collect real times at the process.
- Position yourself so you can see the operator's hand motions.
- Time each work element separately.
- Time several cycles of each work element.
- Observe an operator who is qualified to perform the job.
- Always separate operator time and machine time.
- Select the lowest repeatable time for each element.
- Remember shop floor courtesy.

Operator Balance Chart (OBC) （作業者バランスチャート）

Process:	Product:	Takt Time:	Date/Time:	Notes

① ② ③ ④ ⑤ ⑥ ⑦ ⑧ ⑨

Process									
Time									

Kaizen Express

Example of Operator Balance Chart(OBC) (作業者バランスチャートの例)

Process:	Product:	Takt Time:	Date/Time:	Notes:	Kaizen Workshop #10
Final Assembly #7	AB010	38	Mar. 20.2007		Operator Saving : 1

タクトタイムは
必ず**赤い線**で記入！
Takt Time should be
lined in **red** ink

After Kaizen

Takt Time 38 sec.

	①	②	③	④	⑤
	Assemble1	Forming	Assemble2	Tester	Appr.	Total
	37	36	37	37	37	184

Current Situation

Takt Time 38 sec.

Process	Assemble1	Assemble2	Forming	Assmeble3	Tester	Appr.	Total
	①	②	③	④	⑤	⑥	
Time	38	25	22	33	38	37	193

Kaizen Express

Standardized Work 1: Process Capacity Sheet

(標準作業1：工程別能力表)

Process Capacity Sheet	Approved by:		Part#		Application		Entered by:		Date	
			Part name		Number of parts		Line			
Step	Step Name	Machine#	BASIC TIME		TOOL CHANGE		PROCESSING CAPACITY/SHIFT		Remarks	
			MANUAL	AUTO	COMPLETION	CHANGE	TIME	CHANGE		
			Total							

Kaizen Express

Example of Process Capacity Sheet （工程別能力表の例）

Process Capacity Sheet		Approved by: R. Quan	Part# 25-59001				Entered by: Wayne Xi	Date May 08, 2007
			Application JN-01				Number of parts 1	
			Part name *Base Unit*				Line Machine Shop #2	
Step	Step Name	Machine#	BASIC TIME			TOOL CHANGE		PROCESSING CAPACITY/SHIFT	Remarks
			MANUAL	AUTO	COMPLETION	CHANGE	TIME		
1	Cut	C100	6	32	38	500	2min.	720 p	
2	Rough Grind	GR100	7	12	19	1,000	5min.	1,440 p	
3	Fine Grind	GR200	7	30	37	200	5min.	724 p	
4	Measure Diameter	TS100	8	4	12	—	—	2,325 p	
	Total				28				

The Process Capacity Chart is used to calculate the capacity of each machine in order to confirm true capacity and to identify and eliminate bottlenecks. Processing capacity per shift will be calculated from the available production time, completion time and tool-change time (and other factors as necessary) for each work piece.

工程別能力表は、生産能力を正しく把握してボトルネックを見つけ、改善するために、個々の設備の能力を計算するために使うものです。加工能力は、稼働時間、部品1個あたりの完成時間と刃具交換時間から計算します（必要に応じて、その他の条件を考慮する場合もあります）。

Kaizen Express

Standardized Work 2: Standardized Work Combination Table

（標準作業2：標準作業組み合わせ票）

Standardized Work Combination Table	From:	Date:			Required units per Shift:		Hand
	To:	Area:			Takt Time:		Walk
							Auto

Work Elements	Time (sec.)			Seconds
	hand	auto	walk	5 10 15 20 25 30 35 40 45 50 55 60 65 70 75 80 85 90 95 100
1				
2				
3				
4				
5				
6				
7				
8				
9				
10				
11				
12				
13				
14				
15				
Totals	waiting			5 10 15 20 25 30 35 40 45 50 55 60 65 70 75 80 85 90 95 100
				Seconds

Kaizen Express

Example of Standardized Work Combination Table

(標準作業組み合わせ票の例)

Standardized Work Combination Table	From: *Get work piece*			Date: *April 16, 2007*	Required units per Shift: *550*
	To: *Place finished unit in container*			Area: *Assembly Cell#2*	Takt Time: *49 s*

Work Elements	Time(sec.)			
	hand	auto	walk	Seconds
1 Get circuit board and place in cutter	3	17	1	
2 Get lower case	2			
3 Put circuit into case	4			
4 Get pin & put into case	4			
5 Start machine cycle	1	5	2	
6 Get finished piece	1			
7 Get upper case & put on to finished piece	3			
8 Place into deposit machine & start	3	10	1	
9 Get & check a piece	8			
10 Put into Tester & Start	2	5		
11 Check appearance	5			
12 Put into vinyl bag	3			
13 Place finished unit in container	2		4	
Totals	41 (waiting 0)		8	49

Chart legend: ——— Hand · ∿∿∿ Walk · - - - - Auto

Takt Time — 49 s

The Standardized Work Combination Table shows the combination of manual work time, walk time, and machine processing time for each operation in a production sequence. This form is a more precise process design tool than the operator balance chart. It can be very helpful to identify the waste of waiting and overburden, and to confirm standard work-in-process.

標準作業組み合わせ票を見れば、ラインの作業者ごとに、作業順序に沿って人と機械の組み合わせがどうなっているのかがよくわかります。これは、先に説明した「作業者バランスチャート」よりも精緻な工程設計ツールと言えるでしょう。手待ちのムダやムリを発見したり、標準手待ちを決めるのにも役立ちます。

Standardized Work 3: Standardized Work Chart （標準作業3：標準作業票）

Standardized Work Chart	From:	Date:	Prepared by:	Dept. /Location:	Team Leader:	Supervisor:
	To:					

Quality Check ◇	Safety Precaution ✚	Standard work in process		Takt Time	Cycle Time	Operator Number
		symbol ●	Number of WIP			

Kaizen Express

Example of Standardized Work Chart （標準作業票の例）

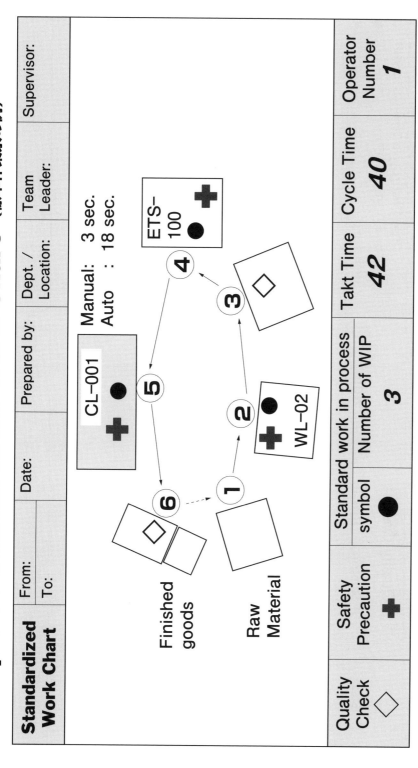

Standardized Work Chart	From:	Date:	Prepared by:	Dept. / Location:	Team Leader:	Supervisor:
	To:					

CL-001

Manual: 3 sec.
Auto : 18 sec.

ETS-100

WL-02

Finished goods

Raw Material

Quality Check ◇	Safety Precaution ✚	Standard work in process		Takt Time	Cycle Time	Operator Number
		symbol	Number of WIP	42	40	1
		●	3			

The Standardized Work Chart shows operator movement and material location in relation to the machine and overall process layout. It should show takt time, cycle time, work sequence and standard WIP.

標準作業票は、作業者の動きと部材の配置と関連付けて表現し、工程全体のレイアウトがわかるようにするのです。タクトタイム、サイクルタイム、作業順序、標準手持ちは、必須です。

Kaizen Express

Standardized Work 4: Job Instruction Sheet （標準作業4：標準作業指導書）

Job Instruction Sheet	Part#		Required Quantity:		Date:		Team Leader:		Supervisor:
	Part name						Prepared by:		

#	Step	Quality Check		Note	Time		Takt Time	Cycle Time	STD WIP	◇ Quality ✚ Safety ● STD WIP
		Sampling	Tool							
					Total					

Kaizen Express

Example of Job Instruction Sheet （標準作業指導書の例）

Job Instruction Sheet	Part#		Required Quantity:	Date:	Dept./Location:	Team Leader:	Supervisor:
	26-0012		**550**	April 26, 2007			
	Part name				Prepared by:		
	Base Unit Assembly						

#	Step	Quality Check			Note	Time	Takt Time	Cycle Time	STD WIP	◇ Quality
		Sampling	Tool				**42**	**40**	**3**	✚ Safety ● STD WIP
1	*Get a work piece and set into fixture*				*With both left and right hand*	*1*				
2	*Remove finished & set new one*					*2*				
3	*Check appearance*	*1/1*	Slide Gauge			*12*				
4	*Remove finished & set new one*				*Clean up head for every cycle*	*14*				
5	*Remove finished & set new one*				*Ensure direction*	*3*				
6	*Check appearance & put into container*	*1/1*	—		*Check both sides*	*8*				
					Total	**40**				

The Job Instruction Sheet is used to train new operators. It lists the steps of the job, detailing any special knack that may be required to perform the job safely with utmost quality and efficiency. It can also be useful for experienced operators to reconfirm them.

標準作業指導書は、新人の訓練に用いるものです。作業手順を書き出し、安全に、良い品質のものを、効率的にこなすための注意点、つまり「急所」を記入します。ベテランの作業者にとっても、注意点を確認するのに役立ちます。

Skills Training Matrix (スキル管理板)

Skills Training Matrix		○ Can do generally ○ Can do well	◐ Certified ● Can do training	Factory name:		Foreman:			
				By:		Date Updated:			
#	Operator Names	Processes						Current Date	Target Date

Kaizen Express

Example of Skills Training Matrix (スキル管理板の例)

Skills Training Matrix		Certified / Can do training	Can do generally / Can do well	Factory name:		Foreman:

Legend: ◑ Can do generally ◑ Can do well ◕ Certified ● Can do training

#	Operator	Cut	Bend	Grind	Weld	Test	Repair	Assem	M.Test	E.Test	Shipping	Current Date	Target Date
1	Mary Li	●	●	●	◔	◔	◑	○	◔	○	○		
		Aug./E			April/E	April/E	April/E						
2	Jerry Quan	◔	◕	◔	◑	◔	◔	○	○	○	○		
		Aug./E	Sept./E	May/E	May/E	June/E	July/E	Aug./E	June/E	May/E	July/E		
3	Sharron Ho	○	○	○	○	○	○	●	●	●	●		
		April/E	April/E	April/E	April/E	April/E	April/E	April/E	April/E	April/E	April/E		
...													

By: _____ Date: _____

The Skills Training Matrix shows the required and attained skills of every operator. The training schedule also should be shown.

スキル管理板は、それぞれの作業者について、必要なスキルと習得済みのスキルを表示するものです。訓練計画も明確にしなければなりません（多能工訓練予定表とも呼びます）。

Kaizen Express

プリント教材
Training Materials

付録−2を第2版で追加しました。読者の皆さんがトレーニングを行う時、「プリント教材」として活用していただければ幸いです。1ページずつなら短時間で説明できるし、何度も繰り返し研究することができるでしょう。

Appendix-2 is new for the Second Edition. We hope you will make copies to hand out during your training. One-page lessons are easy to understand and convenient to pull out to study from time to time.

How do you make a profit?
利益とは？　～原価主義からの脱却～

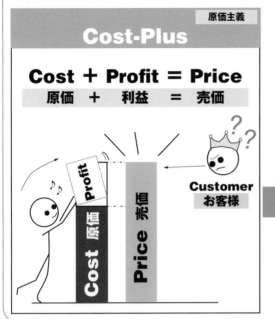

Kaizen Express

利益を出すには？

コストにマージンを乗せて利益を出しますか？
それとも目標の売価を設定し、コストを低減する
ことで利益を出しますか？

原価主義からの脱却

たとえば原価に30％の利益を上乗せして売価を決
める。これが「原価主義」です。しかし、売価を
決めるのは誰でしょう？　お客様ですか？　それ
とも私たちメーカーですか？

利益　＝　売価　－　原価

利益とは売価から原価を引いたものであって、決
して、原価＋利益＝売価ではないのです。この2
つの式は教室で習う数学では同じ意味かもしれま
せんが、私たちが働く人として利益を考える時、
決して「同じではない」のです。

徹底したムダ廃除で原価低減

利益を得るには、原価の中に潜むムダを発見し、
徹底的に廃除し続ける以外に方法はないのです。

How does your company ensure making a profit?

Do you add a margin on top of your cost to
determine your profit? Or, do you set a target
price and then reduce costs in order to ensure
a profit?

Beyond Cost-Plus (Cost + Profit = Price)

Setting the price by adding 30 (or any)
percent to the cost is a kind of "Cost-Plus"
philosophy. But, who should decide the price,
our customer or us, the supplier?

Profit = Price － Cost

Price-Minus thinking means that the profit is
to be induced by subtracting the cost from the
price.　Mathematically, these are the same,
but philosophically they are radically different
and result in very different operational
approaches.

Cost Reduction through Eliminating Waste

We can truly guarantee that we get a profit
only by continuous cost reduction through
identifying and eliminating the waste that is
hidden in the cost.

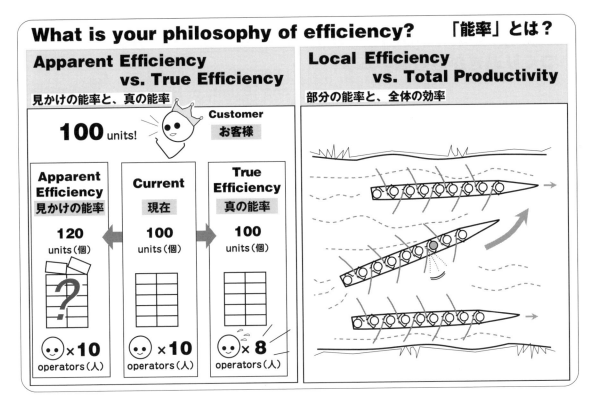

What is your philosophy of efficiency? 「能率」とは？

Apparent Efficiency vs. True Efficiency
見かけの能率と、真の能率

100 units! Customer お客様

Apparent Efficiency 見かけの能率	Current 現在	True Efficiency 真の能率
120 units（個）	100 units（個）	100 units（個）
?		
☺×10 operators（人）	☺×10 operators（人）	☺×8 operators（人）

Local Efficiency vs. Total Productivity
部分の能率と、全体の効率

Kaizen Express

「能率」とは？

工程や人の「能率が良い」あるいは「能率が悪い」とあなたが言う時、それはどんな意味ですか？

見かけの能率と、真の能率

お客様が100個欲しい時に、120個つくって20%の能率アップ。これは「見かけの能率」でしかありません。今10人なら、8人で100個つくれるようになることが、「真の能率」の改善なのです。

部分の能率と、全体の効率

図のまん中のボートはなぜまっすぐ進むことができないのでしょう？　ボートの例ならすぐにわかるのに、私たちは自分の現場の「部分の能率」だけを追い求めてしまいがちです。

What is your philosophy of efficiency?

What do you mean when you say that a process or person is working efficiently or inefficiently?

Apparent Efficiency vs. True Efficiency

Is it efficiency to get a 20 percent increase by producing 120 units when the customer requires only 100 units? True efficiency is to produce the required 100 units with only eight operators when current methods require ten operators!

Local Efficiency vs. Total Productivity

Why is the middle boat not going straight? While we can easily understand the example of the boat, at work we tend to look simplistically for local efficiency rather than total productivity.

Overproduction: The worst form of waste!
つくり過ぎが最も悪いムダ!

Kaizen Express

つくり過ぎに気付こう!

図をじっと見て下さい。どんなムダがあります
か?　つくり過ぎとは何か、皆で話し合ってみま
しょう。

Can you see overproduction?

Look at the chart above. What type of waste
do you see? Talk together about
the waste of overproduction!

つくり過ぎが問題を覆い隠す

つくり過ぎが覆い隠してしまう問題とは何です
か?

Overproduction makes you blind.

What kind of problems do you think might be
concealed by overproduction?

つくり過ぎをやめたらどうなる?

つくり過ぎをやめたら、次の観点から見て、どん
なインパクトがあるでしょう?
—品質は?
—コストは?
—後工程のお客様から見ると?
—自工程の作業者にとっては?
—自工程の監督者にとっては?

What results occur if you stop overproducing?

What impact does preventing overproduction
have on the follow items?
—What about quality?
—What about cost reduction?
—What does it mean to the customer
　downstream?
—How does it impact the operators?
—How does it change what the Team Leaders
　do?

Lead time: Focus your eyes on stagnating time rather than processing time!
リードタイム短縮は、加工時間よりも停滞時間に目を向ける！

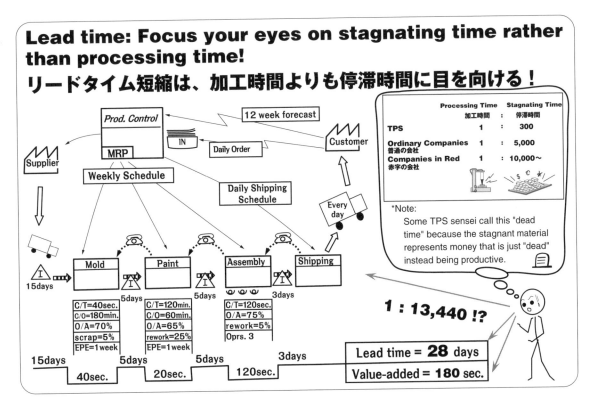

Kaizen Express

加工時間と停滞時間を比べてみれば？！

リードタイムとは、

リードタイム ＝ 加工時間 ＋ 停滞時間

であると言うことができます。

あなたの会社、あなたの生産ラインのリードタイムはどのくらいですか？ 加工時間と停滞時間の比率はどのくらいでしょう？

実際に付加価値を付けている加工時間より、加工されるのを待っているだけの停滞時間のほうがずっと長いことに気付くでしょう。

リードタイムを短縮するには？

したがって、リードタイムを短縮するには、加工時間そのものを短縮しようとするよりも、圧倒的に長い停滞の時間を短縮したほうが、より早く、より大きな効果が得られるのです。

なぜ停滞するのか？

モノの流れが切れているところには必ず停滞があり、停滞があれば積み替えや運搬が必要になります。

Compare processing time and stagnating time!

Lead Time = Processing + Stagnating

How long is the lead time of the product produced on your production line? Of that time, how much is processing time vs. stagnating time?

Usually, much more time is spent stagnating— parts being accumulated before being sent to next process — than being processed.

What should we do to shorten our lead time?

Therefore, we can get a better result quicker by shortening the stagnating time rather than trying to reduce the processing time.

Why do things stagnate?

We have some accumulation everywhere the flow of product is interrupted and we have to load / unload and convey those items to the following processes.

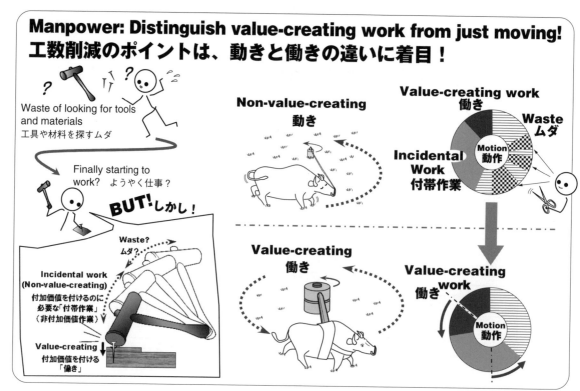

Manpower: Distinguish value-creating work from just moving!
工数削減のポイントは、動きと働きの違いに着目！

Waste of looking for tools and materials
工具や材料を探すムダ

Finally starting to work? ようやく仕事？

BUT！しかし！

Waste?
ムダ？

Incidental work (Non-value-creating)
付加価値を付けるのに必要な「付帯作業」（非付加価値作業）↓

Value-creating
付加価値を付ける「働き」

Non-value-creating
動き

Value-creating work
働き

Waste
ムダ

Incidental Work
付帯作業

Motion
動作

Value-creating
働き

Value-creating work
働き

Motion
動作

Kaizen Express

「働く」とは？

トヨタでは、「働く」とは工程が進み、仕事が出来上がること、とされています。単に「動いて」いるだけではいけないのはもちろん、価値を生み出しながら「工程が進む」ことが不可欠です。皆さんの現場では、どうですか？　「動き」を「働き」に変える改善ができていますか？

付加価値を付けている時間はとても短い?！

たとえば、金槌で釘を打つ時、本当に付加価値を付けているのは、釘が板にめり込む瞬間だけです。

動きと働きの違いに気付こう！

あなたの毎日のすべての仕事を、単なる「動き」と付加価値を付けている「働き」に分けてみましょう。

動きを働きに変える

改善とは、労働強化ではなく、ムダを廃除して単なる動きを働きに変え、人の付加価値を高めることです。

What is work?

In TPS, we think of "work" as only those steps that directly create value. Simply moving is not creating value. How about your gemba? Is your kaizen converting "moving" to "working"?

Actual value-creating time is very short!!

For example, when hammering a nail, the value-creating time is only precisely the instant that the nail is hammered into the board.

Distinguishing work from movement is the first step to eliminate waste!

Separate all of your daily tasks into "movement" and "work."

Convert movement to "work".

Kaizen does not mean the intensification of labor but the conversion of movement to work so all of people's labor can be utilized to create value.

Machines: Do Flow and Motion Kaizen before Machine Kaizen!
設備改善の前にまず工程改善、作業改善！

Flow and Motion Kaizen
工程改善、作業改善

Machine Kaizen
設備改善

Focus directly on the value-creating process.
付加価値プロセスに着目

Isolated processes
工程と工程の間が離れている

Kaizen Express

設備改善はいつ、どのように？

設備改善は非常に重要です。品質や生産性の大幅な改善につながり、また作業者のムリを減らすこともできるでしょう。しかし、設備改善は難しく、また高価なものになってしまう可能性もあります。さらに、設備はモノの流れと人の働きを支えるものでなければなりません。ですから、私たちは、工程改善と作業改善を徹底的に追求した後で設備改善に取り掛かるべきなのです。

まずは設備を工程順に並べるべし！

離れ小島をなくそう！ 離れ小島はムダの元、離れ小島があると、改善が難しくなってしまうのです。

When do you pursue Machine Kaizen?

Machine Kaizen is very important and can lead to big improvements in quality and productivity and can reduce MURI for workers. But, it can also be difficult and expensive. And machines should be configured to support the flow of product and the work of operators. Therefore, we only pursue Machine Kaizen AFTER doing Flow and Motion Kaizen.

Line up machines in a sequential flow.

Eliminate isolated islands! Isolated islands always cause waste and make it hard to do kaizen.

Quality : Inspect products one-by-one immediately at the source process!
「つくったところですぐ検査！」が製造不良ゼロへの道！

- Where and when?
- Who made it?
- How and why?

- いつどこでつくったか？
- 誰が不良をつくったか？
- どうやって、なぜ？

With overproduction and large inventories, you can never spot defects immediately!
不良をつくってしまっても、検査するまでわからない！

Defect!
あー、不良だ！

Final Inspection
分業の検査

Every worker is an inspector!
すべての作業者は検査員！

Never
-accept
-build, or
-pass on
a defect!!

不良は、1つも
- 受け取らない
- つくらない
- 後工程へ流さない！！

Kaizen Express

不良について話し合ってみましょう
— どれだけ早く不良を発見できますか？
— 品質のつくり込みに責任を持つべき人は誰ですか？
— お客様への品質保証はどうやって実現しますか？
— すばやい問題発見と対応をどのように実現しますか？

Talk together about your defects!
— How quickly can you spot defects in your workplace?
— Who is responsible for building in quality?
— How do you ensure perfect quality to the customer?
— How does your work site identify and respond to problem?

分業の最終検査の問題点
最終検査を分業で行っていたのでは、不良を即座に発見することは非常に困難です。また、真因の追究もなかなかできません。それに、製品が最終検査工程に届くまでの間にも、同じ種類の不良をたくさんつくってしまっているかもしれないのです！

Problems of final inspection
It is very hard to find defects immediately by final inspection. It is also difficult to identify the root cause. And by the time the product reaches final inspection, we may have produced many of the same defects!

自工程品質保証を確立しよう！
つくった工程で品質をつくり込み、検査するのなら、不良の発見も、真因の特定も、ずっと簡単にできるようになります。

Ensure your quality at the source process!
It is much easier to find defects and identify their root causes if we build in and inspect quality at each source process.

ワードリスト&索引
Word List & Index

ワードリスト&索引

日本語	英語	参照ページ

日本語	英語	参照ページ
カタカナのムダとひらがなのむだ	waste to be eliminated immediately and waste that cannot be eliminated immediately	12
活動管理板	project tracking board	92
可動率	operational availability	50, 58
稼働率	operating rate	58
かんばん	kanban	33, 40
かんばんのルール	six rules for kanban effectively	42
機械から人を離す	freeing operator from machine	67
機械の見張り	monitoring machines	17, 66
機能別レイアウト	process village layout	29
強制駆動ライン	moving line	50
切り替え	changeover	20, 62, 64
継続的改善	continuous kaizen process	94
限量経営	genryou management	86, 87
工程間の停滞	stagnation between steps (processes)	30
工程間引き取りかんばん	internal kanban, or interprocess kanban	41
工程分析	process study	78
工程別能力表	process capacity sheet	77
個々の能率と全体の効率	local efficiency vs. total productivity	19
固定ロケーション	fixed-location	35

さ

サイクル在庫	cycle stock	47, 82
在庫のムダ	waste of inventory	11
先入れ先出し	FIFO	48
作業	work	11
作業順序	work sequence	76
差し立て板	heijunka box	51
仕掛り	WIP (work in process)	11, 13
実践会	kaizen workshop	16, 91, 92
自働化	jidoka	16, 17, 54, 72
自動織機	auto loom	55, 72
自働杼換装置 (佐吉翁の発明のひとつ)	automatic shuttle changer (pushing-slider)	55
ジャスト・イン・タイム	just-in-time	16, 24
収容数＝入り数 (いりすう)	pack-out-quantity	38, 40, 49, 82
順序生産方式	sequential pull system	46
順序建て	scheduling (only) at the pacemaker	48
少人化	labor linearity	77, 87
省人化	manpower saving, or operator saving	87
少人化ライン → 少人化	flexible manpower line → See "labor linearity".	77, 87

日本語	英語	参照ページ
省力化 ※人手の一部を機械に置き換えることができたものの、省人化できない状態を意味する言葉。本書では紹介していない。	labor saving ※Labor saving means partial replacement of manual labor by machines. It also means it is not the extent of one operator saving. This term is not explained in this book.	
真因	root cause	60, 61
シングル段取り	SMED（Single Minute Exchange of Die）	64
スーパーマーケット	supermarket	33, 35
スキル管理板	skills training matrix board, or plan for every employee	20
生産管理板	production analysis board	30, 81, 83
生産指示かんばん	production kanban	41
製品部群別整流化レイアウト	process sequence layout by product family	29
設備改善	right-sized equipment, right-sized tooling, improvement of machine	19, 88
設備総合効率	Overall Equipment Effectiveness ［OEE］	59
設備の6大ロス	six major losses in machinary	59
外段取り	external setup work	64, 65

た

日本語	英語	参照ページ
大量生産	mass production	17
タクトタイム	takt time	13, 25, 26, 76, 81
多工程持ち	multi-process handling	17, 67
多台持ち	multi-machine handling	17, 56, 67
多能工	multi-skilled operator	19
段階的設備投資	capital linearity	87, 88
段取り改善	setup reduction	62
段取り替え	setup	64
段取り時間	changeover time	26, 62
チャクチャク	chaku-chaku	68
注文頻度	order frequency	33
使うところ	point-of-use, or consuming process	37, 40
つくったところ	supplying process	35
つくり過ぎ	overproduction	10, 13
つくり過ぎのムダ	waste of overproduction	10, 13, 32
提案制度	suggestion program	91
定位置停止	fixed-position stop system	74
定時不定量	fixed time, unfixed quantity	34
停滞	accumulation, stagnation	12, 25
停滞のムダ	waste of accumulation	12
定量不定時	fixed quantity, unfixed time	34
徹底したムダ廃除	eliminating waste thoroughly	14
手待ちのムダ	waste of waiting	10
動作のムダ	waste of motion	11
時計回り	clockwise	38
豊田喜一郎	Toyoda, Kiichiro	15

日本語	英語	参照ページ
豊田佐吉	Toyoda, Sakichi	15
トヨタ生産方式	Toyota Production System	14
トヨタ生産方式の2本柱	two pillars of the Toyota Production System	14
ドロッパー（佐吉翁の自動織機の縦糸切断自動検知・自動停止機構）	dropper（to stop automatic loom）	55

な

流れ	flow	29
流れ化	continuous flow	25, 28, 50
流れ棚	flow rack, or sloping parts rack	38
にんべんのついた自働化	jidoka with human touch	54
ネック工程	bottleneck process	48
納入指示かんばん	supplier kanban	41

は

拍動	pace	48
バッチサイズ	batch size	49
バッファ在庫	buffer stock	47, 82
離れ小島	isolated island（isolated process）	31
ハネ出し	auto eject	57, 66, 68, 69
反時計回り	counter-clockwise	38
日当たり平均所要	average daily demand	47
引き取り	pull	32
	withdrawal	33
引き取りかんばん	withdrawal kanban	41
ピッチ	pitch	38
必要なものを、必要なときに、必要なだけつくり、提供する	making and delivering what is needed, just when it is needed, and just in the amount needed	24
人の仕事と機械の仕事を分ける	separating human work and machine work	16, 54, 66
1人完結	produce with only one operator; only one operator makes the product from beginning to end	31
人を尊重する	respecting people	97
ひもスイッチ	signal cord	50, 73
標準作業	standardized work	76
標準作業組み合わせ票	standardized work combination table	77
標準作業指導書	job instruction sheet	77
標準作業票	standardized work chart	77
標準手持ち	standard in-process stock, or standard WIP	76
フォード式	Fordism	28
付加価値を生まない作業	non-value-creating work	11, 31
付加価値をつける働き	value-creating work	11

日本語	英語	参照ページ
付帯作業	incidental work	11
部品の置き方	parts presentation	30
不良ゼロ	zero defects	72
不良をつくるムダ	waste of correction, waste of defects	11
分業型レイアウト	process village layout, or job shop layout	29
平準化	heijunka	24, 44
ペースメーカー	pacemaker	47, 48
可動率	operational availability	50, 58
変動係数	demand variation	47
ポカヨケ	error-proofing（device）	73
補充	replenishment	33

ま

日本語	英語	参照ページ
前工程	upstream process, or upstream operation	32
まとめ生産	batch production	44
見える化	visualization	82
見かけの能率と真の能率	apparent efficiency vs. true efficiency	18
水すまし	mizusumashi, or material handler using very frequent withdrawal and delivery	33
店　→　スーパーマーケット	supermarket	33, 35
ムダ	waste	10, 12
むだ	waste（that cannot be eliminated immediately）	12
ムダの廃除	elimination of waste	12
ムラ	fluctuation, or unevenness	12
ムリ	overburden	12
目で見る管理	visual management	80
もったいない	mottai nai	57

や

日本語	英語	参照ページ
よい品　よい考	Good Products, Good Thinking ※"Good Thinking, Good Products" と訳されることも多い。本書ではオリジナル表現を尊重。	91

ら

日本語	英語	参照ページ
乱流まとめ生産	batch-and-queue	29
ロットを小さく、段取り替えを速やかにして（モノをつくる）	producing smaller batches with quick changeover	62

Word List & Index

English	Japanese	参照ページ

English	Japanese	参照ページ

E

eliminating waste thoroughly	徹底したムダ廃除	14
error-proofing（device）	ポカヨケ	73
external setup work	外段取り	64, 65

F

five Whys	5回のなぜ	60
fixed-location	固定ロケーション	35
fixed-position stop system	定位置停止	74
fixed quantity, unfixed time	定量不定時	34
fixed time, unfixed quantity	定時不定量	34
fluctuation	ムラ	12
Fordism	フォード式	28

G

| genryou management | 限量経営 | 86, 87 |
| Good Products, Good Thinking | よい品　よい考 | 91 |

H

| heijunka | 平準化 | 24, 44 |
| heijunka box | 差し立て板、(負荷)平準化ボックス | 51 |

I

internal kanban, or interprocess kanban	工程間引き取りかんばん	41
internal setup work	内段取り	64
isolated island（isolated process）	離れ小島	31

J

jidoka	自働化	16, 17, 54, 72
jidoka with human touch（automation with a human touch）	にんべんのついた自働化	54
job instruction sheet	標準作業指導書	77
just-in-time	ジャスト・イン・タイム	16, 24

English	Japanese	参照ページ

English	Japanese	参照ページ
pitch	ピッチ	38
PM（Preventive Maintenance）	PM	59, 60
point-of-use	使うところ	37
poka-yoke	ポカヨケ	73
process capacity sheet	工程別能力表	77
process study	工程分析	78
process village layout, or job shop layout	分業型レイアウト、機能別レイアウト	29
production analysis board	生産管理板	30, 81, 83
production kanban	生産指示かんばん	41
pull system	後工程引き取り	25
push	押し込み	32

R

English	Japanese	参照ページ
replenishment	後補充、補充	33
replenishment pull system	後補充生産方式	46
right-sized equipment, right-sized tooling	流れの中で使える設備、設備改善	19, 88
root cause	真因	60, 61

S

English	Japanese	参照ページ
safety factor	安全係数	47
safety stock	安全在庫	47, 82
separating human work and machine work	人の仕事と機械の仕事を分ける	54, 66
sequential pull system	順序生産方式	46
setup reduction	段取り改善	62
seven wastes	7つのムダ	10
signal cord	ひもスイッチ	50, 73
six major losses in machinary	設備の6大ロス	59
six rules for kanban effectively	かんばんのルール	42
skills training matrix board	スキル管理板	20
SMED（Single Minute Exchange of Die）	シングル段取り	64
stability	安定化	25
stagnation between steps（processes）	工程間の停滞	30
standard in-process stock, or standard inventory	標準手持ち	76
standardized work	標準作業	76
standardized work chart	標準作業票	77
standardized work combination table	標準作業組み合わせ票	77
supermarket	スーパーマーケット、店、ストア	33, 35
supplier kanban	納入指示かんばん	41

T

English	Japanese	参照ページ
takt time	タクトタイム	13, 25, 26, 76, 81
Toyoda, Kiichiro	豊田喜一郎	15

English	Japanese	参照ページ
Toyoda, Sakichi	豊田佐吉	15
Toyota Production System	トヨタ生産方式	14
TPM（Total Productive Maintenance）	TPM	59, 60
TPS（Toyota Production System）	TPS（トヨタ生産方式）	14
two pillars of the Toyota Production System	トヨタ生産方式の2本柱	14

U

English	Japanese	参照ページ
unevenness	ムラ	12
upstream process, or upstream operation	前工程	32
U-shape	U字型	31

V

English	Japanese	参照ページ
Value Stream Mapping	Value Stream Mapping	26
value-creating work	付加価値をつける働き	11
visual management	目で見る管理	80
visualization	見える化	82

W

English	Japanese	参照ページ
waste	ムダ	10, 12
waste（that cannot be eliminated immediately）	ひらがなのむだ	12
waste of accumulation	停滞のムダ	12
waste of conveyance	運搬のムダ	11
waste of correction, waste of defects	不良をつくるムダ	11
waste of inventory	在庫のムダ	11
waste of motion	動作のムダ	11
waste of overproduction	つくり過ぎのムダ	10, 13, 32
waste of processing, waste of overprocessing	加工そのもののムダ	11
waste of waiting	手待ちのムダ	10
WIP（work in process）	仕掛り	11, 13
withdrawal kanban	引き取りかんばん	41
work in process	仕掛り	11, 13
work sequence	作業順序	76

Z

English	Japanese	参照ページ
zero defects	不良ゼロ	72
zone control	自工程品質保証	72

読者の皆さんへ─あとがきに代えて
Postscript

1999年の秋、"Learning to See" の日本語版出版のため、わたしたちは、東京で話し合う機会を得ました。その時の会話から生まれた着想が、時を経て本書につながっています。めぐり合わせの不思議を思わずにはいられません。

わたしたちは、どのような文化圏でも、どのような組織でも、トヨタ生産方式を正しく学び、実践するのなら、そこで働く人々とその組織に根源的な変化をもたらすことができると確信していました。そのためには、かたちのあるもの、ないものも含めて、いろいろなものが必要ですが、それぞれが簡単には手に入らないうえに、相互に関連し合ってもいるために、スタート地点ですべてを揃えることができる組織は皆無に近いでしょう。「何が必要か？」「どうすればそれを得られるか？」ということは、当時も今もわたしたち共通の関心事です。たとえば「トップのリーダーシップ」は、いつもリストの最初に挙げられますが、お金を出して買えるものでないことは明白です。「結局のところ、意識の問題だ」という表現も、最も頻繁に登場する言葉のひとつです。その通り、トップ・マネジメントから従業員一人ひとりに至るまで、人々の意識改革なしに真の変革を起こすことはできません。しかし、人々の意識を変えるには、どうすればよいのでしょう？

読者の皆さんと同じく、わたしたちがトヨタのやり方から学んだことは数え切れませんが、意識についてなら、第一に、明確な目標を持たねばならないこと、真の意識改革は実践のなかからしか生まれないこと、加えて、意識改革の停滞は後退と同義である、ということを、まず言わなければならないでしょう。おそらく本書の読者の皆さんは、このことを実感として知っているはずです。

人々の意識を変えることは、かの如く困難である。しかし、そうであるからこそ、「正しい実践の方法」を知ることには大きな意味がある。よりよい意識改革は、より正しい実践のなかから生まれるのだから！　それが、当時のわたしたちが考えていたことの一つでした。「技法や手法よりも、まず意識！」「知識は後からついてくる」と誰もが言い、また実際その通りであることが多いのですが、同時に、正しい知識の欠落が改革の停滞を招いているケースが少なくないことも、わたしたちは知っていました。

正しい実践の方法を正しく伝えるためにLEIが企画したツール・キット・プロジェクトの最初の成果が "Learning to See" です。多くの人々の助力を得て、日本でその翻訳版が世に出たのが1999年の暮でした。それから6年、LEIのツール・キットとして一連のワークブックが整い、もう教科書はこれ以上要らないという気分でもあった2005年夏、成沢が「普通の日本人が使える英語の教科書がない」と言い出し、日本の月刊誌・工場管理で連載を始めます。LEIの成果を引用しながら、日本人が海外で使うための日英対訳の基本教材としてまとめなおそうという試みでした。

わたしたちがTPSを学び始めてから今日まで、たどってきた道はそれぞれに異なっていますが、多言語環境下でTPSを考え、人々の改善を助ける仕事をしてきたという意味ではいくつかの共通点

があります。シュックは、1980年代前半から90年代にかけてトヨタ本社で働き、日本語でTPSを学びました。トヨタで、シュックは、NUMMIの多くのアメリカ人達に日本のトヨタの考え方を教えるため、TPSそれ自体と教材群を海外へ持っていくのを支援するという仕事を経験します。後に、シュックは、トヨタのケンタッキー工場で指導する日本人トレーナーに対し、TPSやその他のことがらについてどのように「英語で」コミュニケーションすべきかを教える仕事にも携わり、トヨタを離れる90年代前半までに、1,000人を超えるトヨタの人々にTPSを教えることになりました。一方、成沢はNECに勤務していた80年代末にTPSを学び始め、後には英語で表現されたTPSを勉強して海外工場の人々に改善を伝えるための方法を研究するようになります。探求の途上、"Learning to See"の翻訳を通して、トヨタグループの外側にいる日本の人々に、バリュー・ストリーム・マッピングという一種の共通言語があることを知らせるきっかけをつくることができたのは幸運でした。

本書の単行本化に際し、シュックが成沢の試みを応援しようと決めたのは、トヨタグループ以外の日本企業の人々にとってそれが必要であることを、よく知っていたからです。わたしたちが8年前に思い描いていた「基本事項をきちんと織り込んだシンプルな本」に近いものになったのはうれしいことです。しかし、その一方で、本書が、トヨタの人材育成について深く触れることができなかったことを反省しなければならないでしょう。TWI（Training Within Industry）をはじめとする基礎的な訓練の重視はもちろんのこと、個々の部門での日々の仕事のやり方からトップ・マネジメントに至るまで、トヨタでは、一人ひとりに責任を持たせ、考えさせ、実行させ、反省を促して再び次の改善に向かわせるというサイクルが止まることはありません。毎日の仕事のなかで人の能力を常に開発するということは、トヨタの人々にとっては空気であり、水なのです。トヨタを離れてから、新たな企業や組織と出会うたび、シュックはそのことを何度も思い返してきました。

わたしたちは、この領域、つまり、人の能力を引き出す枠組みや風土、それを支える教育訓練についても、さらに研究を続けたいと考えていますが、それは現場の改善から離れて成り立つものではないはずです。現場から学ぶことを繰り返しながら、わたしたちは、自分自身を見ることを学んできたのだと改めて思います。おそらく、読者の皆さんも同じような経験をされてきたことでしょう。わたしたちは、皆さんが、世界各地の現場で新しい発見を続けられるよう願っています。本書が、何らかの形でその助けとなることができるなら、これに勝る喜びはありません。

2007年7月

成沢俊子、ジョン・シュック

参考文献

Bibliography

※日本の書籍は、本書発行時点で英訳本が存在するものを紹介しています。

- 大野耐一、1978年、トヨタ生産方式―脱規模の経営をめざして、ダイヤモンド社
  英訳　Toyota Production System : Beyond Large-Scale Production, Productivity Press, 1988

- 大野耐一、2001年 (1983年版の新装版)、大野耐一の現場経営、日本能率協会マネジメントセンター
  英訳　Workplace Management, Productivity Press, 1988
  2001新装版の英訳本は下記にて入手可
  Workplace Management, translation by Jon Miller, Gemba Press, 2007
  (Only available in Kaizen Products Store ; http : //gembapress.com/)

- Harris, Rick ; Harris, Chris ; and Wilson, Earl, 2003. *Making Materials Flow*.
  Lean Enterprise Institute.

- Marchwinski, Chet, and Shook, John, compilers. 2006. *Lean Lexicon*. (*Third Edition*)
  Lean Enterprise Institute.

- Rother, Mike, and Shook, John. 1998. *Learning to See*.
  Lean Enterprise Institute.
  邦訳：トヨタ生産方式にもとづく「モノ」と「情報」の流れ図で現場の見方を変えよう!!
  2001年8月　日刊工業新聞社

- Rother, Mike, and Harris, Rick, 2001. *Creating Continuous Flow*.
  Lean Enterprise Institute.

- Smalley, Art. 2004. *Creating Level Pull*.
  Lean Enterprise Institute.
  邦訳：トヨタ生産方式にもとづく『ちょろ引き』で生産管理を改革しよう!!
  2006年10月　日刊工業新聞社

- Womack, James, and Jones, Daniel, 1996. *Lean Thinking*.
  Simon & Schuster.
  邦訳：リーン・シンキング、稲垣公夫訳 (「ムダなし企業への挑戦」の改題)
  1997年6月　日経BP社 (2003年改題)

- Womack, James, and Jones, Daniel, 2002. *Seeing the Whole*.
  Lean Enterprise Institute.

著者紹介
About the Authors

著者：成沢　俊子 (なるさわ　としこ)

1983年～2002年 NECに勤務。金融庁勤務を経て、PEC産業教育センターにて改善を研究。人間環境大学非常勤講師。"Learning to See"「トヨタ生産方式にもとづく『モノ』と『情報』の流れ図で現場の見方を変えよう!!」(2001)、"Creating Level Pull"「トヨタ生産方式にもとづく『ちょろ引き』で生産管理を改革しよう!!」(2006)（ともに日刊工業新聞社）の翻訳者。

協力：John Shook (ジョン・シュック)

Lean Enterprise Institute シニア・アドバイザー。TWI Network, Inc.代表、Lean Transformation, LLC.代表。ミシガン大学 Japan Technology Management Program　前 Director。1983年、最初の外国人正規社員としてトヨタ本社に入社、後にトヨタ本社初の米国人課長となる。Toyota North American engineering & R&D center 総務部長、Toyota Supplier Support Center 副所長を経て、現職。主な著書に"Learning to See"他。

新装版「工場管理」基本と実践シリーズ
英語でkaizen！ トヨタ生産方式
2023 年 1 月 27 日　初版 1 刷発行

Ⓒ著　者　　成沢　俊子 with John Shook
　　発行者　　井水　治博
　　発行所　　日刊工業新聞社
〒103-8548　東京都中央区日本橋小網町14-1
　　電話　　03-5644-7410（販売・管理部）
　　　　　　03-5644-7490（書籍編集部）
　　FAX　03-5644-7400
　　振替口座　00190-2-186076
　　　URL　https://pub.nikkan.co.jp/
　　e-mail　info@media.nikkan.co.jp
　　印刷・製本　美研プリンティング